Invitation to the Torah

Invitation to the Torah

A Guide to Reading, Teaching, and Preaching the Pentateuch

GEORGE VAN PELT CAMPBELL

with Derek Van Pelt Campbell

WIPF & STOCK · Eugene, Oregon

INVITATION TO THE TORAH
A Guide to Reading, Teaching, and Preaching the Pentateuch

Wipf & Stock
An Imprint of Wipf and Stock Publishers
199 W. 8th Ave., Suite 3
Eugene, OR 97401

www.wipfandstock.com

PAPERBACK ISBN: 978-1-7252-7749-6
HARDCOVER ISBN: 978-1-7252-7748-9
EBOOK ISBN: 978-1-7252-7750-2

Manufactured in the U.S.A.   07/01/20

John Passmore said,
any writing "is made possible only by a series of 'graces,' gifts from others, gifts the author has done nothing to deserve. . . . For an author to feel proud of himself for what he has done would be absurd. In relation to any single one of these graces he is, no doubt, a co-operator: no one of them, by itself, explains why he has written as he has written. . . . A deeper exploration of the situation, however, soon reveals how dependent even [his] 'originality' is on other sources of grace, on genetic inheritance, on upbringing."

I dedicate this book
to the memory of my father and mother,
George Edward and Constance Van Pelt Campbell
Whose love, support, faith, integrity and love of the life of the mind
Introduced me to all of the core "graces"
Which have made me what I am;
and to my wife
Karen Campbell
Dearest friend and loyal companion
Who has continued the grace in ways without number
And filled my life with indescribable richness;
And to my daughter
Joanna Campbell-Totin
With love and gratitude for her proofreading and editorial help
On numerous writing projects.
And to my son Derek Van Pelt Campbell
With love and gratitude for his assistance on this book.

Contents

Acknowledgments

I wish to express my gratitude to the Board of Trustees and Administration of Grove City College in Grove City, Pennsylvania, for granting me a sabbatical during the Fall semester of 2020, during which the bulk of the research and writing was done. My thanks is particularly extended to Dr. Paul McNulty, College President, Dr. David Ayers, Acting Provost, Dr. Paul Kemeny, Acting Dean, Dr. Peter Frank, Provost, and to the Committee members who granted the sabbatical. I was also grateful to be working at home when the COVID-19 virus spread globally. I am grateful to my Department Chair, Dr. Seulgi Byun, for his support of the project and for shouldering my Assistant Chair duties during the sabbatical in the midst of an already demanding schedule. Finally, I am grateful to my colleagues in Biblical and Religious Studies at Grove City College for their encouragement and support of the project.

I also wish to express sincere thanks to my family. My wife, Karen, has been very supportive of the project from the beginning and encouraged me to apply for the sabbatical. Without her, the book would not have come about. My daughter, Joanna, has once again applied her considerable proofreading and editing skills, and I am grateful for her eye for detail and her suggestions. Finally, I am grateful for the assistance of Derek Van Pelt Campbell, my son. He is the primary author of chapter 9 on Deuteronomy, on which he preached for nearly a year, and for many other suggestions which improved the book. It was a pleasure to have him contribute to this project. I am also grateful to Dr. Jeff Patterson and to my Student Assistant, Charlotte Ebert, for making helpful suggestions.

Abbreviations

AB	Anchor Bible
ANE	Ancient Near East
BECNT	Baker Exegetical Commentary on the New Testament
DOTP	*Dictionary of Old Testament: Pentateuch*, edited by T. Desmond Alexander and David W. Baker. Downers Grove, IL: InterVarsity, 2003.
IBC	*Interpretation: A Bible Commentary for Teaching and Preaching*
JSOT	*Journal for the Study of the Old Testament*
JSOTSup	Journal for the Study of the Old Testament: Supplement Series
JPSTC	Jewish Publication Society Torah Commentary
LXX	Septuagint
NAC	New American Commentary
NICOT	New International Commentary on the Old Testament
NICNT	New International Commentary on the New Testament
NIDOTTE	*New International Dictionary of Old Testament Theology and Exegesis*, edited by Willem A. VanGemeren. 5 vols. Grand Rapids: Zondervan, 1997
NIVAC	The NIV Application Commentary
NT	New Testament
OT	Old Testament
OTL	Old Testament Library

PTW	Preach the Word Series, edited by R. Kent Hughes
TOTC	Tyndale Old Testament Commentaries
WBC	Word Biblical Commentary

Introduction

Reading the Torah, the first five books of the Bible, is about as exciting as watching paint dry! At least, that is the view of about 99 percent of Christians. Yet there is a minority report from those who have spent a lot of time reading the Torah. Many would probably vote that someone who enjoys Deuteronomy is well-described by the slander aimed at Paul, "your great learning is driving you out of your mind" (Acts 26:24). But what if those who know the books most broadly are those whose perspective is most perceptive? Could it be that a little knowledge of the Torah is a dangerous thing, that lack of familiarity is what breeds contempt?

Augustine voiced the minority report in the fifth century when he wrote that the Bible is like the ocean: it is shallow enough for a child to paddle in but also deep enough for an elephant to drown in.[1] (The "shallow" part is the majority report!) The purpose of this book is to convince you that the beginning of the Bible is the most important, most significant, most relevant thing in it. I am not a prophet, nor the son of a prophet, but I know what you are thinking: "Mission Impossible!" I hope to persuade that when I say the Torah is as beautiful as a sunset it is not because I've lost my mind, but because I've gained my sight by studied attention.

The journey of a thousand miles begins with a single step, as the Chinese proverb says. The journey in this book involves several steps. First, I must bring you to see that Genesis, Exodus, Leviticus, Numbers, and Deuteronomy are not a collection of ancient *laws* (the majority report) but a continuous *story*. I compare it to the *Star Wars* saga. I will also show you that those "books" are one big book, and that it is the fountainhead of the rest of the Old Testament. We will see that the Old Testament was rearrangement by Christians but that the original Jewish ordering demonstrates that the

1. See Duguid, *Numbers*, 16.

Torah contains the primary Old Testament message. These things constitute Part 1, the Primacy of the Torah.

Part 2 is the core of the book. I take you through each "book" of the Torah (Genesis, etc.) and determine its message. Since the Torah is fundamentally about getting to know God, I compare it to the richest human experience of deeply knowing someone else, that is, courtship, marriage, and living happily ever after.

Part 3 of the book presents a comprehensive statement of the message of the Torah. After presenting its principles, I illustrate the message as the Torah itself does, by comparing and contrasting the two most famous people in the Torah story. Their biographies *show* the Torah message in human experience.

Part 4 aims to equip you with aids to read, teach, or preach the Torah.

My goal is to reveal the message of the Torah and explain how it develops across the five units so that you can dive in and read it with understanding. I am convinced that it contains all the key lessons of the Bible. The rest of Scripture expounds and elaborates the Torah.

If the Bible is God's book, you'd expect him to be able to produce something at least as interesting and rich as Shakespeare or J. K. Rowling. Multitudes of Christians have testified over many centuries that God did indeed do so. I hope what I have said here will entice you read this book, and then with its help, read the Torah, believing that God would not have given us a book without profit or reward. Like all good things, that profit does not always come easily. So, I challenge you to do the work to go beyond paddling in the shallows and take the plunge to swim in the depths. I believe you will find it worth the effort. Knowing God more deeply and intimately is the prize. The adventure awaits!

Chapter 1

Invitation to the Torah

Four half-score and seven years ago, roughly, the first *Star Wars* film was released. I was a first-year seminary student in 1977 when *Star Wars: A New Hope* introduced my wife and me to Luke, Han Solo, Princess Leia, Chewbacca, and C-3PO. We anticipated three episodes, then were pleased when we learned that three more were coming! We met Obi-Wan Kenobi, Qui-Gon Jinn, Padme Amidala, and Anakin Skywalker. We never believed we would see the last three episodes that were originally announced, but—wonder of wonders, miracle of miracles—we finally got to meet Rey, Finn, and Kylo Ren. We saw each one and enjoyed following the tale. We loved the adventure (would Han be freed from the carbonite?), the suspense ("is it true that a Jedi can't be killed?"), the surprises (who was Luke's father?), and the drama of good versus evil (could Darth Vader turn?). *Star Wars* is a grand story told in nine action-packed episodes that kept us engaged for over forty years.[1]

The Torah, the opening section of the Jewish Bible, is also a grand story, but one told in five drama-filled episodes. These books, Genesis, Exodus, Leviticus, Numbers, and Deuteronomy are called the "Pentateuch" ("book with five parts") by Christians. But we will use its original name. Like *Star Wars*, the Torah covers a series of generations, tracing a continuous story. It has heroes and villains and people in between. It portrays people who display heroism and courage and those who fight for justice. It also showcases

1. The comparison with *Star Wars* I owe to my son, Rev. Derek Van Pelt Campbell.

the greedy, the self-serving, and the base. Further, like *Star Wars*, it bears witness to a great power, above and around us all. But it is not an impersonal Force; it is a personal God, who loves and seeks out people to establish a relationship with them. Also, unlike the Force, the God of the Torah is not balancing good and evil. Instead, he is wholly good, hating evil. Paradoxically, this God deeply loves the people he created, yet who have partaken of the "dark side" (that's all of us, in degrees). He is someone devoted to rescuing us from the dark side, which is the plot of the Torah's grand story. So, early in the story (Genesis 3:15) he promises that he will defeat the dark side and put the world right.

Even more exciting, this adventure is not just a spectator sport! Unlike *Star Wars*, this is a real-life drama in which the God of the Torah invites us all to participate (and not just Jews!). He welcomes all who are willing to join the fight against the evil empire and to work to restore the noble republic. It's an invitation to join the winning side of history's greatest drama.

In order to demonstrate these things, we will begin our journey by asking and answering four questions in this chapter. What sort of literature is the Torah? Is it one book or five books? What subdivisions are there in the Torah? Does the Torah have a message?

WHAT SORT OF LITERATURE IS THE TORAH?

The first question is "What sort of literature is the Torah?" Getting this right can draw you in like the smell of freshly baked bread, or it can put you off like the smell of burnt toast.

Law or Instruction?

Most people think of the Torah as "Law." While it is true that the Hebrew word *torah* is often properly translated "law," its basic meaning is "instruction." The Torah contains stories and poetry interwoven with laws, but the first laws, the Ten Commandments, or Ten Words[2] do not occur until Exodus 20. So, a third of the Torah is written before any laws are given![3] The Torah is not a "law book," but instruction which includes some laws. Who

2. Christians have long termed them the "Ten Commandments," but the Jews have always termed them the "Ten Words" which is what the Bible actually calls them. This is because many of them are, in Hebrew, one word, preceded by the Hebrew word "not"/"no"/"Do not," e.g., "Not murder," "Not adultery."

3. In the standard printed Hebrew Bible, the Torah is 353 pages long. Genesis 1–Exodus 19 is 133 pages, or 33 percent of the Torah.

wants to read law books except lawyers? That would make the Torah more like burnt toast. But an instruction manual about something you are interested in (like getting to know God) is more like fresh bread.

Law or Stories (Narrative)?

We have seen that the function of the Torah is to provide instruction, but what type of literature is it if it is not legal literature? The answer is that it is narrative literature—stories! This may sound counterintuitive, so let's demonstrate it. Fee and Stuart point out that Genesis is largely narrative and that Exodus and Numbers also contain substantial narrative portions.[4] But Wenham also notes that "Leviticus is essentially a narrative work."[5] Leviticus is mostly priestly rules and regulations, yet Wenham is correct for at least two reasons. Leviticus continues the story of Genesis and Exodus. For example, Exodus 25–40 is mostly about the tabernacle and the garments and ordination instructions for the priests who serve in it. But the actual ordination of the priests is not described until Leviticus 8–10, thus continuing the Exodus story. The second reason Wenham is correct is that nearly every chapter is introduced by "the Lord spoke to Moses," or a similar phrase; this reminds us that this is continuing the story of Moses.[6] Deuteronomy is similar. It is essentially Moses' story brought to completion as he gives his parting instructions to Israel in the last two or three days of his life. So, the Torah is fundamentally a long story with Moses as a central figure.[7]

So, like *Star Wars*, the Torah is a long story. It is a multigenerational drama about how God deals with people, establishing the Bible's instruction about how we relate to God. The more we think of it as a story the more we will want to read it. Freshly baked bread!

IS THE TORAH ONE BOOK OR FIVE?

Our second question is whether the Torah is one book or five books? The Torah is the opening section of the Christian Old Testament, or the Jewish "Hebrew Bible." It now consists of five books: Genesis, Exodus, Leviticus, Numbers, and Deuteronomy. In fact, even in Jesus' day (roughly AD 0; we

4. Fee and Stuart, *How to Read*, 93. Dillard and Longman call Leviticus "instructional history" (*Introduction*, 75)

5. Wenham, *Pentateuch*, 81.

6. Wenham, *Pentateuch*, 81.

7. We will argue later that Abraham and Moses are the two key figures who are presented as a study in contrasts.

don't know the actual date!), thinking of the Torah as five books was an ancient tradition. It dates at least as far back as the Septuagint (the translation of the Hebrew Bible into Greek, beginning about 250 BC). But it is indisputable that the Torah was originally one book.[8] We will briefly provide the evidence for this, but the takeaway is important: since the Torah is *one book*, we must read it as a whole and seek its message by considering all of it. *The Empire Strikes Back* is not the whole story.

So, how do we know that the Torah was written as one book? Most importantly, references to it in the Bible are *always* in the singular. For example, just after Moses' death, Joshua refers to the Torah (Joshua 1:7–8): "Only be strong and very courageous, being careful to do according to all the law [Hebrew *torah*] that Moses my servant commanded you. Do not turn from it to the right hand or to the left, that you may have good success wherever you go.[9] This *Book of the Law* shall not depart from your mouth, but you shall meditate on it day and night" (emphasis added). The New Testament does the same. For instance, Mark reports that Jesus said (Mark 12:26), "And as for the dead being raised, have you not read in the *book of Moses*, in the passage about the bush, how God spoke to him, saying, 'I am the God of Abraham and the God of Isaac and the God of Jacob'?" (emphasis added). The Torah is also one continuous narrative, as we'd expect in a single book.[10] Then, near the end of the Torah we read that Moses "finished writing the words of this law in a book [singular] to the very end." (Deut 31:24). Finally, there is no evidence of any division of the Torah until late, in the second century BC.

ARE THERE SUBDIVISIONS IN THE TORAH?

Our third question is, are there subdivisions in the Torah's structure? That is, if the Torah was originally one book, why is it now five books? Like a single man in possession of a good fortune being in want of a wife, the answer is a truth universally acknowledged.[11] While the Torah was written as one book, it was composed with five distinct subunits that correspond to

8. Sailhamer argues this in his *Pentateuch*, 1–2; so does Wenham, *Pentateuch*, 5. He also points out that why and when it was split into five books is lost in the mists of time.

9. I once knew a Dean of Students who said at Freshman Orientation, "Look to your left, look to your right, your future mate may be in sight." The exhortation to Joshua has more gravity because the stakes are higher.

10. See Wenham, *Pentateuch*, 5.

11. This allusion to *Pride and Prejudice* I owe to Joanna Campbell-Totin.

the five "books" into which the Torah was eventually divided.[12] When the Torah was eventually divided into the five "books" with which we are so familiar (when, by whom, and why we don't know), they correctly sensed the distinct subunits into which Moses divided his book.

We will now demonstrate this by showing that each of the five books of the Torah displays a clear internal structure that distinguishes it from the other units and establishes its own internal limits. Since this is not controversial, we can summarize this material briefly.[13]

Genesis

Genesis is often divided into topical units: the primeval history (Genesis 1–11), Abraham (Genesis 12–25), Isaac and Jacob (Genesis 26–36) and Joseph (Genesis 37–50). This is accurate and useful.[14] But this organization by content/people is not the outline that the author wrote for his audience to notice. Remember that biblical books were written in an oral culture, to be read out loud since very few people could read. The writer outlined Genesis by a phrase that the audience could hear repeated. The phrase is "these are the generations of."[15] The term "generations" (*toledot*) is derived from the Hebrew verb *yalad*, "to give birth," and can refer to a genealogy (e.g., Genesis 36:1; 36:9). But the first time it is used, the author signals that he will not necessarily use it that way. In Genesis 2:4 he wrote, "These are the generations of the heavens and the earth" (Gen 2:4). Note that "the heavens and the earth" *do not* give birth and the phrase *is not* followed by a genealogy. The phrase is used metaphorically. In many cases Moses[16] follows the

12. Since the subunits are regularly called "books," we will use that terminology here for convenience.

13. Childs treats the evidence in *Introduction*, 128–31; see also LaSor et al., *Old Testament*, 54.

14. The subunits are actually, respectively, Gen 1:1–11:26; 11:27–25:18; 25:19–37:1; 37:2–50:26. It is important to remember that the chapter and verse divisions that are now used worldwide were not part of the original text, and were added for convenience many, many centuries after the Scriptures were completed. Both chapter and verse schemes were done independently in many places for both the OT and the NT, and the ones which prevailed date from the ninth to sixteenth centuries: OT verses, c. AD 900; OT chapters, *either* AD 1244 or 1330; NT chapters in AD 1227 by Stephen Langdon, later Archbishop of Canterbury; NT verses in AD 1551 in Robert Stephanus's Greek New Testament. See Bruce, *Books*.

15. This structural device is widely acknowledged, e.g., Wenham, *Pentateuch*, 18; Childs, *Introduction*, 145.

16. The issues around the idea that Moses is the author of the Torah will be explored below.

phrase with a series of stories that describe the development and eventual fate of a thing or (usually) a person. In other words, the phrase means "this is what became of [X]."[17] The NIV translates, "This is the account of." After Genesis, *toledot* ceases to function as a structural marker. This yields the following structure:

- Creation story: 1:1—2:3 (not a *toledot* unit)
- The *toledot* of the heavens and the earth: Gen 2:4—4:26
- The *toledot* of Adam: Gen 5:1—6:8
- The *toledot* of Noah: Gen 6:9
- The *toledot* of Shem, Ham and Japheth: Gen 10:1
- The *toledot* of Shem: Gen 11:10
- The *toledot* of Terah: Gen 11:27
- The *toledot* of Ishmael: Gen 25:12
- The *toledot* of Isaac: Gen 25:19
- The *toledot* of Esau: Gen 36:1, 9
- The *toledot* of Jacob: Gen 37:2

Exodus

"There is no series of genealogical formulae to provide clearly marked divisions."[18] Exodus is generally outlined in three sections by its contents, as follows[19]:

1. Exodus 1–18: The exodus from Egypt
2. Exodus 19–24: God gives Israel his law
3. Exodus 25–40: The tabernacle

So, Exodus is distinct from Genesis, as well as from Leviticus below.

17. Merrill et al., *Word and World*, 173.
18. Childs, *Introduction*, 170.
19. Wenham, *Pentateuch*, 58; also Dillard and Longman, *Introduction*, 62.

Leviticus

Wenham states, "Leviticus is characterized by clear organization. Titles mark the beginning of new sections and summary formulae mark section endings. By and large the chapter divisions, introduced into the Bible in the Middle Ages, pick up these earlier division markers correctly."[20] The organization and the holiness[21] theme distinguish the book. Wenham's (abbreviated) outline:[22]

1. Leviticus 1–7: Laws on sacrifice and the priesthood
2. Leviticus 8–10: Institution of the priesthood
3. Leviticus 11–16: Uncleanness and its treatment
4. Leviticus 17–27: Prescriptions for practical holiness

Numbers

Wenham comments, "Unlike Genesis and Leviticus, whose structure is clearly marked by recurring formulae, Numbers runs on as a continuous narrative, so that it is not clear exactly how it should be divided."[23] Olson provides the best picture of the Numbers's framework:[24]

1. Numbers 1–25: The old generation of rebellion
2. Numbers 26–36: The new generation of hope

Deuteronomy

Deuteronomy stands as a distinct unit in the Torah. It's structure became widely recognized in the twentieth century. It follows the form of a Hittite treaty from about 1400 BC, when Moses lived.[25] These "suzerain-vassal" treaties had a specific set of elements in a specific order at different times during the two millennia of Hittite ascendancy. The treaty document

20. Wenham, *Pentateuch*, 81–82, is representative. See also Wenham, *Leviticus*, 50.

21. See, for example, Ross, *Leviticus*, which is also a very useful guide to passage-by-passage understanding.

22. Wenham, *Pentateuch*, 81–82.

23. Wenham, *Pentateuch*, 103.

24. Olson, *Numbers*, 3–7, the outline stated on 5–6.

25. E.g., von Rad, *Deuteronomy*, 21–23; Craigie, *Deuteronomy*, 20–29, Merrill, *Deuteronomy*, 22–23.

informed the servant people (the "vassal") of what their king (the "suzerain") expected of them:

- Preamble: Deut 1:1–5
- Historical prologue: Deut 1:6—4:40
- General stipulations: Deut 5:1–33
- Specific stipulations: Deut 6:1—26:15
- Blessings and curses: Deut 27:1—28:68
- Historical review Deut 29:1—30:20)
- Deposit and reading: Deut 31:1–29
- Witnesses:
- Moses' song as witness: Deut 32:1–47
- Heavens/earth as witness: Deut 4:26, 30:19, 31:28; 31:19

Although Moses utilizes the suzerain-vassal treaty form, he modifies it at several points in line with his aims.[26] We conclude that the five books of the Torah are distinct units, corresponding to the five books in Christian Bibles. Like the numerous songs of Andrew Lloyd Webber's *Phantom of the Opera*, each component of the Torah plays a distinct role in the story.

IS THERE A MESSAGE IN THE TORAH?

While a book can instruct through laws or principles, Moses did not choose that form of instruction. Instead he told a five-part, multi-generational story to tutor Israel and us. Does it have a unified message? That it is called "instruction" suggests so. But if it walks like a duck and quacks like a duck, it's a duck. So, finding what looks and sounds like a unified message is the proof. We allege that the Torah incorporates the main message needed by God's people of all time.[27] The Torah establishes the plot of the rest of the Old (and New) Testament story.

Since Moses wrote five units, we will briefly summarize his argument that way.

26. For example, he changes the witness to the treaty from the gods of the region to the heavens and the earth, moves the blessings and curses to follow the specific stipulations, and adds an historical review near the end.

27. Although Christians do not live under the Mosaic Covenant, the Torah, along with all Scripture (2 Tim 3:16) is profitable for the Christian because it reveals God's heart and character. Chapters 10 and 11 develop this idea.

Genesis: God created the world as a house where he could live with his people and bless them with abundant life; when sin brought death into his house, God began fulfilling a promise to restore life out of death.

Exodus: To restore abundant life, God initiated a plan like marriage, in which he courted a people, invited them to commit themselves to him, and when they said, "I do," built a house so he could live with his people.

Leviticus: Because living happily ever-after involves many adjustments, God established a plan so that his bride could live in intimate contact with him and deal with anything that might alienate them from each other, and created ways for her to grow ever closer to him so they could share abundant life.

Numbers: Each generation of God's people must choose to remain faithful over the long haul, choosing unbelief and disobedience with its tendency toward death (loss of blessing) or faith and obedience with its tendency to enhance life (God's rich blessing).

Deuteronomy: Loving the Lord and obeying his good rules brings life and personal and social well-being.

The Torah's message summary (Deut 30:19–20): "I have set before you life and death, blessing and curse. Therefore, choose life, that you and your offspring may live, loving the LORD your God, obeying his voice and holding fast to him, for he is your life and length of days."

In a nutshell, that is the argument of the Torah, expressed through the key themes of life and death. We will see that it is also the argument of the entire Old Testament. Certainly, the failure of Israel to obey the Mosaic Covenant necessitated a New Covenant (see Jeremiah 31:31–32) which Jesus inaugurated. That New Covenant nuanced and modified the particulars of how God deals with his people. But the Torah argument stands as the Bible's *foundational instruction* for God's people for all time. As Paul wrote, referring to the events in the Torah, "Now these things happened to them as an example, but they were written down for our instruction, on whom the end of the ages has come" (1 Corinthians 11:10).

Chapter 2

The Torah Gave Birth to the Hebrew Bible

We have argued that the Torah has a message and that that message is the core of the Bible's instruction for God's people of all ages. This implies that the Torah is the fountainhead of the rest of the Old Testament. This chapter will show that the Torah gave birth to the rest of the Old Testament Scriptures.

The Torah established conditions that required further Scripture; this is clear from the forward-looking nature of the Torah. In brief, the argument is that because the Torah made promises that were unfulfilled by its end, more Scripture from inspired prophets was necessary to chronicle the fulfillment of God's sure promises made in the Torah.[1] We will see this in three complementary ways: (1) the Torah's focus on the latter days, (2) the forward-pointing nature of the Torah's end and (3) the continuation of the Torah's forward-pointing orientation at the end of the Hebrew Bible.[2]

1. Beale's discussion of the nature of unfulfilled prophecies (direct and indirect) in the Old Testament in his *Handbook* sparked my reflection upon this issue, but he does not treat its implications for the canon of Scripture. Merrill begins his discussion of the theology of Genesis by describing its "eschatology" (forward-pointing nature): Merrill, *Biblical Theology*, 16; Childs also refers to the "eschatological framework" of Genesis (i.e., it's forward-looking nature) and develops the importance of promise in Genesis (*Introduction*, 58, 150–52).

2. The Genesis genealogies contribute to this (DeRouchie, Blessing-Commission, 240): "The driving, in-motion nature of the linear genealogies identifies them with the book's forward-looking, hope-filled theme."

THE TORAH HAS AN "END-OF-DAYS" FOCUS

Like objects hidden in plain sight, it is not commonly noticed that there is a strong focus in the Torah on (what the Hebrew calls) "the end of days."[3] The phrase occurs four times in the Torah, though translations render them differently: Genesis 49:1, Numbers 24:14, Deuteronomy 4:30 and 31:29. Three of the uses (all but Deut 4:30) occur as the introduction to a prophetic speech written in poetry which describes the end of history.[4] The Hebrew Bible thus begins with the Torah holding the listener's attention on the end of history when the Torah's promises will be entirely fulfilled. However, the three passages introduced by "what will happen in the end of days" do more than focus on the future. Each one also predicts the coming of a great king who will come in the end of days. Like a movie that returns to the same music each time a theme or character appears, the Torah calls attention to the end-of-days king by repeating this phrase.

The first use of "the end of days" is in Genesis 49:1 and is part of a larger phrase, "what will happen in the end of days." Here Jacob speaks prophetically about the future of each of his twelve sons, who will become the fathers of the twelve tribes of Israel. He starts with the oldest son and works to the youngest, giving the blessing—or otherwise—appropriate to each one based upon their character and behavior in the Genesis stories. Some of the prophetic utterances recorded here obviously relate to the immediate future, but the phrase "the end of days" specifies that the complete fulfillment of at least some of these will not occur until history's end.

Sailhamer[5] appears to have been the first scholar to observe that in three of the cases (all but Deut 4:30), the phrase "the end of days" is embedded in a larger, complex prose introduction to a lengthy piece of poetry. The prose introduction in each case consists of five parts that are virtually identical in the Hebrew. The repetition of these five elements makes it clear that the author intended the second and third occurrences as allusions, i.e., to remind the listener of the first. The ancient audiences would have noticed the nearly identical repetition in the three texts.. In each case the central figure in the narrative at that point (Jacob, Balaam, and Moses, respectively) calls together an audience and says to them, roughly, "Let me tell you what will happen to you in the end of days" (with three elements in the Hebrew that are virtually identical). This repeated flourish signals to the reader the importance of what follows. The fact that what follows is written in poetry further highlights its

3. Sailhamer expounds this in both his *Pentateuch* and *Meaning*, and Beale also develops this at length in *New Testament Theology*, 88–116.

4. This phrase is the source for Paul's NT descriptions of the "last days" (2 Timothy 3:1).

5. Sailhamer, *Pentateuch*, 35–37; See also Waltke, *Theology*, 151–55.

importance. The author wants the audience to compare and contrast the three passages (Genesis 49, Numbers 24, and Deuteronomy 32–33).

When we observe the three long and very different poems which follow the common introduction, what stands out is that "the end of days" in each case is said to include the coming of a king. Here are the texts about the king (emphasis is added):

Genesis 49:10: "The *scepter* shall not depart from *Judah*, nor the ruler's staff from between his feet, until tribute comes to him; and to him shall be the obedience of the peoples."

Numbers 24:17: "I see him, but not now; I behold him, but not near: a star shall come out of Jacob and a *scepter* shall rise out of Israel; it shall crush the forehead of Moab and break down all the sons of Sheth."

Deuteronomy 33:5–7: "Thus the LORD became king in Jeshurun [i.e., Israel], when the heads of the people were gathered, all the tribes of Israel together. . . . And this he said of Judah: 'Hear, O LORD, the voice of *Judah* and bring him in to his people.'"[6]

The Genesis (Genesis 49:8–12) promise is the first and primary text. The two later texts key off of it and repeat and develop aspects of that foundational text.[7] The prophecy regarding Judah predicts victory over his enemies (Gen 49:8a), which is reiterated in Numbers 24:14 and Deut 33:7. Numbers 24:9 quotes Genesis 49:9. Gen 49:8b states that Judah's brothers "shall bow down before" him, clearly an allusion to the promise made in a dream to Joseph (Gen 37:7). In other words, the triumph and authority that Joseph experienced will be reflected in the king who will eventually arise from the tribe of Judah. But Joseph's rule over one nation will be gloriously overshadowed when the king from Judah reigns over "the people," i.e., the nations of the world, in "the end of days"! Genesis 49:10 says, "the scepter will not depart from Judah" until tribute comes to the one to whom it belongs. This tells us that every king from the tribe of Judah who would reign in Israel was to be a foreshadowing of *the* king who would someday come and completely fulfill the prophecy (though many failed miserably!). The Psalmist reflects on the ultimate fulfillment of the Genesis promise in Psalm 2:6–8, where God says of the messianic king, "I have set my king on Zion,

6. Deuteronomy 33:1–7 is often seen as difficult to interpret; see Craigie, *Deuteronomy*, 390–94 and Merrill, *Deuteronomy*, 435–37. But it clearly is an elaboration upon Genesis 49:10, as Craigie (*Deuteronomy*, 393), and Merrill acknowledge (*Deuteronomy*, 437). Sailhamer argues that 33:7 should be translated, "Hear, O Lord, the voice of Judah, and bring to his people the one who contends with his own hands for what belongs to him." I.e., the prayer is for the king promised to Judah (Gen 49:10) to come to Israel. Sailhamer, *Meaning*, 468–71.

7. See Sailhamer, *Pentateuch*, 234–36.

my holy hill . . . . Ask of me and I will make the nations your heritage and the ends of the earth your possession." So, does Daniel 7:13–14: "there came one like a son of man and he came to the Ancient of Days and was presented before him. And to him was given dominion and glory and a kingdom, that all peoples, nations and languages should serve him; his dominion is an everlasting dominion, which shall not pass away and his kingdom one that shall not be destroyed." Revelation 5:5, 9, agrees: "behold, the Lion of the tribe of Judah, the Root of David, has conquered. . . . And they sang a new song, saying, 'Worthy are you to take the scroll and to open its seals, for you were slain and by your blood you ransomed people for God from every tribe and language and people and nation.'" Note that "Lion of the tribe of Judah" is derived from Genesis 49:9.

So, the prophecies in these three Torah passages speak of the line of kings who will come from the tribe of Judah. They also look forward to a final fulfillment that will transcend even David, Judah's greatest king, because he fell short of the full predictions given here. Thus, the Torah songs about the coming king push the reader to focus beyond the Torah itself to the "end of days" when *the* king from Judah will exercise an everlasting dominion (Isaiah 9:6–7). The Torah songs are like classical music that replays the same theme with variations.

Notice that these poems are expounding a poem in Genesis 3:15. God says to the serpent after our first parents eat from the forbidden tree, "I will put enmity between you and the woman and between your offspring and her offspring; he shall bruise your head and you shall bruise his heel." This cryptic verse has (rightly) been taken as the first announcement of the gospel ("*protoevangelium*"). Notice its structure:

- "Enmity between you and the woman" = the *individuals*
- "and between your offspring and hers" = the *line* of descendants from each
- "*he* shall bruise . . . bruise *his* heel" = future *individual* heir from Eve.

Next note that the structure of Genesis 49:10 is parallel to Genesis 3:15, showing that the author is developing 3:15 in 49:8–10 and its context. Genesis 49:10 says:

- "Judah, your brothers shall praise you" = the individual
- "scepter will not depart from Judah" = the *line* of descendants (the tribe of Judah)
- "until *he* comes" = future *individual* heir from Judah.

So, the forward-looking focus of the Torah begins early (Genesis 3) and is held regularly before the reader (Genesis 49, Numbers 24, Deuteronomy 31–33). From the very start, the Torah continually reminds the reader to look to the future, beyond the Torah itself, for the coming king. If the godly are to do what the Torah urges, more inspired prophets and more Scripture from them must come to trace the development of the Torah promises to their final conclusion.

THE TORAH ENDS POINTING THE READER FORWARD

The second and most important indication that the Torah established conditions that required further Scripture is found in the forward-pointing nature of the Torah's end. Deuteronomy covers the last few days of Moses' life, and consists largely of speeches Moses gave as his parting instruction to Israel. Like President Washington bidding farewell to his countrymen after two presidential terms, Moses takes his leave of his people, passing the mantle to others and imploring them to heed his distilled wisdom for their future. The book contains several forward-looking elements. Deuteronomy 18:15–18 records a particularly important one that God revealed to Moses: "The LORD your God will raise up for you a prophet like me from among you, from your brothers—it is to him you shall listen. . . . I will put my words in his mouth and he shall speak to them all that I command him." This promise means two things.[8] It predicted a line of prophets who would follow Moses and who would be "like" Moses in providing divine guidance to future generations of Israel.[9] This prophecy came true in Isaiah, Jeremiah, and the other prophets. The Jewish name for the books immediately following the Torah is "the Prophets,"[10] as we will see later. That is, the Jewish community saw the fulfillment of the promise of Deuteronomy 18 in the prophets who wrote the history (Joshua, Judges, Samuel, Kings) and the prophetic oracles (Isaiah, Jeremiah, Ezekiel and The Twelve) that comprise the next major section of the Hebrew Bible after the Torah.[11]

8. Craigie, *Deuteronomy*, 262–63. Merrill observes, "This order was first spoken of in the singular. . . . The ambiguity of the individual and collective both being expressed in the grammatical singular is a common Old Testament device employed to afford multiple meanings, or applications, to prophetic texts" (*Deuteronomy*, 272).

9. See also Levinson, *Jewish Study Bible*, 408, note on Deut 18:15, "The continuity of prophecy is assured. . . . *A prophet*, while grammatically singular, is distributive in its meaning: 'I will repeatedly raise up for you a prophet.' More than one prophet is clearly intended." See also Craigie, *Deuteronomy*.

10. This will be clarified in the next chapter.

11. Dempster, *Exploring*, 99.

But there is more to the meaning here, a second meaning indicated by Deut 18. Christians have long seen Deut 18 as also pointing to Messiah.[12] How can this be justified? The reason is that Moses predicted a prophet "like Moses" (18:15, 18). What was to follow was not simply prophets, but prophets "like Moses." The words "like Moses" seem to indicate people of the character, stature and greatness of Moses. Moses is portrayed in Scripture as the prophet *par excellence*, part of which we see here because all future prophets are to be compared to him and measured by whether they measure up to him. Some of those characteristics are stated in the following paragraph (speaks in God's name, predictions come true: 18:19–22), but "like Moses" is the prime characteristic. This interpretation is confirmed by the last words of the book, Deuteronomy 34:10–12. Notice that the phrase "like" Moses is used twice in Deut 34:10–12, mirroring the same double-use in Deut 18:15, 18. "And there has not arisen a prophet since in Israel like Moses, whom the LORD knew face to face, none like him for all the signs and the wonders that the LORD sent him to do in the land of Egypt, to Pharaoh and to all his servants and to all his land and for all the mighty power and all the great deeds of terror that Moses did in the sight of all Israel." As we will argue in the next chapter, a later inspired prophet appended these words to Moses' book after the gift of prophecy had ceased. Two observations deserve note: he interprets "like Moses" to mean "as great as Moses," and he declares that no one ever measured up, indicating that the prophecy of Deut 18:15–18 was never fulfilled. The forward-looking perspective here assumes prophecy has ceased, which the Jews acknowledged as having occurred with Malachi. Thus, the end of the Torah pushes the reader to seek *the* prophet *after the completion of the entire Hebrew Bible*. Christians identify Jesus as that prophet.

These observations point to another and astonishing realization: since the end of Deut also points to prophetic writings *beyond the Hebrew Bible*, a Christian can argue that the end of Deut thus established the need for the New Testament. That additional revelation would trace the Torah promises beyond the Old Testament! The evidence suggests that the apostles who wrote the New Testament thought exactly this way.

Consistent with what we have argued, "over the course of time, the verses concerning the prophet came to be recognized within later Judaism as having a future and prophetic point of reference."[13] We see abundant evi-

12. Levinson, *Jewish Study Bible*, 408, comments, "A much later Jewish reinterpretation that was accepted by the Christian church (John 1.21, 34; 6.14; 7.40; Acts 3.22; 7.37) understands the verse to promise a single, messianic prophet at the end of time." While some Christians have seen it as either-or, it is now widely seen as both-and.

13. Craigie, *Deuteronomy*, 263.

dence of this in the New Testament. When John the Baptist came, people asked him, "Are you *the* Prophet?" (John 1:21). Note that John's contemporaries are still looking for "*the* prophet" Moses predicted.[14] Peter quoted Deut 18 and argued that Jesus was its fulfillment (Acts 3:19–24). So, Jesus' apostles saw Jesus as the final fulfillment of the prediction in Deut 18. The New Testament Scriptures were written to explain that this was the case. So, while Jesus authorized the New Testament Scriptures,[15] that authorization was already in the Torah. The Torah established the need for Scripture after the Old Testament.

THE CONTINUATION OF THE TORAH'S FORWARD-POINTING ORIENTATION IN THE HEBREW BIBLE

The third indication that the Torah established conditions that required further Scripture after the Torah is found in the Hebrew Bible's continuation of the Torah's forward-looking perspective. We will learn in the next chapter that the Hebrew Bible is arranged differently than the Christian Old Testament. Some inspired prophet arranged the completed Old Testament books into three sections called the Law, the Prophets, and the Writings. This final author of the form in which the Hebrew Bible has come down to us apparently saw the Torah's future orientation and added endings to the Prophets and the Writings to maintain the Torah's forward-looking thrust in the entire Hebrew Bible.

The Prophets end urging the reader forward in Malachi 4:5–6: "Behold, I will send you Elijah the prophet before the great and awesome day of the LORD comes."[16] The "day of the Lord" is the day of judgment at "the end of days," often referred to by the prophets. Elijah may be specified here as a representative of all the prophets, or perhaps because he was seen as the closest to a "prophet like Moses." But what matters is that the Prophets end pushing the reader to the future. This again implies that more prophets must supply more Scripture to chronicle the final fulfillment of the Torah's promise of *the* prophet like Moses. Like a newscaster saying, "Stay tuned for details as this story develops," Malachi ends with, "stay tuned."

The Writings likewise end with a forward-looking word. Israel's exile is yet to end at the conclusion of Chronicles and the Writings end with the

14. The Greek is clear here in saying "the prophet," not "a prophet."

15. Texts normally cited include John 14:26, 15:26–27, 16:12–15.

16. There is a dispute about whether "Elijah" here is "the messenger" of Malachi 3:1 (likely so), and whether the prophecy here is fully fulfilled in John the Baptist (Matthew 17:10–13) or not. These disputes do not affect our argument.

words of 2 Chronicles 36:23: "Thus says Cyrus king of Persia, 'The LORD, the God of heaven, has given me all the kingdoms of the earth and he has charged me to build him a house at Jerusalem, which is in Judah. Whoever is among you of all his people, may the LORD his God be with him. Let him go up.'" Though it seems unusual to us, the Writings end the Hebrew Bible looking forward to the future return to Israel. So, "the book thus ends with the possibility of a new exodus. . . . Chronicles thus ends with the promise that the people of God would again go free to build a sanctuary where they could worship him in the land he had promised to their ancestors."[17]

We have seen that the Torah itself established the conditions that called for more Scripture from inspired prophets after the Torah was completed. It did so through a general forward-looking stance, which looked beyond its time toward the "end of days." It also did so through a prediction of more prophets to come after Moses laid down that mantle (Deut 18:15–18) and a surprising statement that that prophecy was never fulfilled during the centuries when the gift of prophecy was given (Deut 34:10–12). Then the Prophets and the Writings end as the Torah had ended. They push the reader beyond their inspired writings to future writings and a future time when God's sure Torah promises will be fulfilled. The fact that the Torah gave birth to the Prophets and the Writings and even to the New Testament is powerful evidence that the Torah is the heart of the Hebrew Scriptures. It also shows that the Prophets and the Writings were composed to explain and expand upon the Torah. To the justification of this claim we now turn.

17. Thompson, *Chronicles*, 400.

Chapter 3

Jesus' Bible was "Tanak"

Like cleaning up a messy room, Christians have long loved to avoid picking up the Pentateuch.[1] In fact, if they were honest, Christians would admit that they think that "Leviticus" is the definition of "dull," and that they marvel that a book named "Numbers" was ever written at all! This is to say nothing (which is usually the case!) of dusty old Deuteronomy. The reality is that apart from some stirring passages here and there, the Torah is largely an opaque book for most Christians. A few Christian preachers graze through Genesis, or perhaps examine the edges of Exodus, but after that, even for pastors, the eyes glaze over and slumber settles in.

This is especially interesting because Jesus loved Deuteronomy as Mr. Spock loved logic. It was Jesus' favorite book.[2] He knew it so well that he could quote three appropriate passages from memory when he faced temptation in the wilderness (Matthew 4; Luke 4) and it was the only book he relied upon to sustain him in that ordeal. It's also interesting in light of the fact that the Torah is almost 20 percent of the entire Christian Bible.[3] Further, Christian disinterest in the Torah is striking in light of the fact that the New Testament contains approximately 1000 quotations from and allusions

1. "Pentateuch" is Greek, and means "five scrolls," and became the Christian term for the Torah about the third century AD because Greek was the widespread language of the Roman Empire when Christianity began.

2. If we judge by how often he quoted from the Scriptures: see Block, *Deuteronomy*, 26. One can argue for other books as Jesus' favorite, e.g., Isaiah.

3. It is 17 percent of the Bible.

to the Torah.[4] That averages three or four references to the Torah per page of the New Testament! It also means, on average, that every page of the Torah (about 200 pages long in the Christian Bible) is cited five times in the New Testament![5] For a Christian to ignore the Torah is like snubbing your sweetheart's favorite music.

So, it will be as shocking as a nudist in church that the contention of this book is that the Torah is the heart of the Hebrew Bible (the "Old Testament"),[6] and that the rest of the Old Testament was written to explain and expand the Torah. It is essentially the case that everything you need to know is in the Torah! This does not mean that Old Testament Scripture after the Torah is unimportant. Far from it! But it means that its conscious purpose was not fundamentally to give new revelation (though it does that) but to elaborate upon the Torah.

To establish this claim, we will show in this chapter how the Jewish arrangement of the Hebrew Bible differs from the Christian ordering of the books. Then the next chapter will show that the intent of the Jewish order was to teach the primacy of the Torah.

TANAK: THE JEWISH ARRANGEMENT OF THE HEBREW BIBLE

Since long before the Christian era, the Hebrew Bible had an established arrangement which the Jewish community has maintained to the present today.[7] The Hebrew Bible (in the Hebrew language) that contemporary Christian scholars also use is arranged in this form and has been since Christian scholars returned to study of the Old Testament in Hebrew in

4. This count is an estimation from the data provided in the appendix to Aland et al., *Nestle-Aland Greek Text*, 739–47, and compared with Aland et al., *Greek New Testament*.

5. It also means that while the Torah is 22 percent of the Old Testament, it is the source of 31 percent of all quotations and allusions from the OT.

6. Merrill writes that the Pentateuch "is universally regarded by both the Jewish and Christian traditions as being foundational to whatever else the Old and New Testaments say theologically. . . . these books are the fountainhead of theological inquiry": *Biblical Theology*, 7–8. Yet, while Christian scholars say so, few average Christians, or even pastors, think in those terms.

7. Bruce notes, "It has frequently been suggested that, while the canon of the Palestinian Jews was limited to the twenty-four books of the Law, Prophets, and Writings, the canon of the Alexandrian Jews was more comprehensive. There is no evidence that this was so: indeed, there is no evidence that the Alexandrian Jews ever promulga-ted a canon of scripture." Bruce, *Canon*, 44–45.

the late fifteenth century.[8] Like a long-lost uncle, the Hebrew arrangement of the books is only unfamiliar to Christians because of lack of exposure. Early Christians rearranged the order of the books; why, we do not know.

The Jewish arrangement of the Hebrew Bible is called "Tanak."[9] This is what is printed on the cover or the spine of a Hebrew Bible (i.e., a Jewish Bible in Hebrew) rather than "Holy Bible." "Tanak" is an acronym for the first letter of the name of each of the three sections of the Hebrew Bible, as FBI is an acronym for "Federal Bureau of Investigation," or ASAP means, "As Soon As Possible." TNK stands for "T*orah*," N*ebi'im*," and "K*etubim*," the Hebrew words for "Law," "Prophets," and "Writings." To pronounce TNK, an "a" vowel is inserted between the consonants. While the content of the Hebrew Bible is the same as that of the Christian Old Testament,[10] the order of the books is different.[11]

The Jewish order of the Hebrew Bible books in Tanak is listed below, grouped under the traditional categories.[12] The Jewish Prophets contains books that Christians think of as historical books (the "Former Prophets," though there is a series of prophets mentioned in them)[13] and Daniel is included in the Writings. "The Twelve" are what Christians call "The Minor Prophets." An asterisk (*) indicates books written as a unified whole which were later divided, for reasons unknown.

8. From the completion of Jerome's Latin Vulgate (405 AD), until 1488, when the first printing-press printed edition for the Bible in Hebrew appeared, Christian scholars studied the Old Testament in Latin.

9. Sometimes "Tanakh," or "TNK," or TaNaK," etc.

10. To be precise, the content of the *Protestant* Old Testament is identical with the Hebrew Bible. The Roman Catholic Old Testament contains additional material, historically called the "Apocrypha," which the Jews never accepted as Scripture. For discussion, see Bruce, *Canon*, 15–114 and Beckwith, *Canon*. During the period of the Reformation, Protestants affirmed their acceptance of only those books included in the Jewish canon of Scripture, while Roman Catholicism formally declared (at the Council of Trent, 1563–65) what had long been affirmed by many Christians, that the apocryphal books were to be regarded as part of Old Testament Holy Scripture.

11. Some Christians have utilized the Tanak order, e.g., Harrison, *Introduction* and Childs, *Introduction*.

12. While Christians count the number of Old Testament books as 39, the Jews have traditionally counted them as 24 (sometimes as 22, by combining Ruth with Judges and Lamentations with Jeremiah). The larger Christian number derives from the eventual separation of several of the books, Samuel, Kings, Chronicles and Ezra-Nehemiah into 2 each (= 24 + 4 = 28), and counting The Twelve as twelve instead of one, adding 11 more to the count (=28 + 11 = 39). By the time that the number 24 is attested, the Torah was already numbered as five books.

13. See Dempster, *Exploring*, 100.

- **Torah*** (The Law [of Moses])
- Genesis
- Exodus
- Leviticus
- Numbers
- Deuteronomy

- **Nebi'im** (The Prophets)
- *The Former Prophets*
- Joshua
- Judges
- Samuel*
- Kings*

- *The Latter Prophets*
- Isaiah
- Jeremiah
- Ezekiel
- The Twelve

- **Ketubim** (The [Sacred] Writings, sometimes "Hagiographa," Latin for "Sacred Writings")
- *Poetry*
- Psalms
- Job
- Proverbs

- *The Megollith ("The Five Rolls")*
- Ruth
- Song of Solomon

- Ecclesiastes
- Lamentations
- Esther

- *Historical Books*
- Daniel
- Ezra-Nehemiah*
- Chronicles*

TANAK PREDATES THE TIME OF CHRIST

Basis in the Hebrew Bible

Like buggy whips, the arrangement of the Hebrew Bible is ancient: Tanak predates the time of Christ. There are indications within the Hebrew Bible itself that at least later authors saw God's revelation as of three sorts.[14] Jeremiah wrote, "Then they said, 'Come, let us make plots against Jeremiah, for the *law* shall not perish from the priest, nor *counsel* from the wise, nor the word from the *prophet*'" (18:18, emphasis added). Similarly, Ezekiel wrote of those who "seek a vision from the *prophet*, while the *law* perishes from the priest and *counsel* from the elders" (7:26, emphasis added). The three types of revelation named by both authors as law, counsel, and prophecy correspond to Tanak's Law, Prophets, and Writings (associated with wise counsel). It is reasonable to suggest that these categories gave birth to three units of Scripture.

Early Evidence for Tanak

The earliest evidence of Tanak outside of the hints in the Hebrew Bible is from the apocryphal[15] book of Ben Sira, a Jewish document dated ca. 180 BC.[16] In 39:1 the author declares of the wise man, "How different the man

14. See Dempster, *Exploring*, 92.

15. The apocrypha is a group of books included in the Roman Catholic Old Testament but not the Protestant one.

16. Ben Sira is included in the Catholic Old Testament. It is also called "Sirach" and "Ecclesiasticus."

who devotes himself to the study of the *law* of the Most High! He explores the *wisdom* of the men of old and occupies himself with the *prophecies*."[17] Here we see the same three-part division of revelation into law, prophecy and wisdom, expressed by Jeremiah and Ezekiel, though the order varies in the three authors.[18] But about 132 BC[19], Ben Sira's grandson wrote a prologue to his grandfather's work when he translated it into Greek for publication. Three times in his prologue, he refers to a three-part division of revelation, clearly seeming to be restating the three-part division stated by his grandfather. But in each case he states them in the order in which Tanak has come down to us. Here we see for the first time the three-part division of the Hebrew Bible stated in the order in which it has remained ever since.[20] So, there is good evidence that since at least ca. 132 BC and perhaps before 180 BC, the Jewish community conceived of the Hebrew Bible as Tanak.

CHRISTIANS CHANGED THE JEWISH ORDER OF THE BOOKS

When Greek became the most widely-know language and Hebrew had ceased to be well-known among the Jews, the Jewish community in Alexandria, Egypt, decided to render their Scriptures into Greek. This translation came to be known as the Septuagint ("seventy," and abbreviated by "LXX").[21] The Torah translation began about 250 BC and the rest was completed over time. The Septuagint became the Jewish Bible used in synagogues and eventually also the Old Testament of the early Christian church. The Greek New Testament documents were added to it by Christians to create a Greek Bible. It is in the Septuagint that we first encounter the Old Testament in a form different than Tanak. Unfortunately, the earliest complete copies of the Septuagint we possess come from the fourth and fifth centuries AD and are Christian books and the order of the books is different in each one.[22] So, we are unable

17. Emphasis added; cited from *New American Bible*.

18. See Dempster, *Exploring*, 110–11.

19. Bruce, *Canon*, 31.

20. Further attestation comes from a Qumran document, 4QMMT, dated sometime from the mid-second century BC to the late first century BC, which speaks of "the Book of Moses [and] the Book[s of the P]rophets and Da[vid]," and from Josephus in his *Against Apion* 1:37–43, where he writes of five books of Moses, thirteen Prophets and "the rest of the books," and other sources as well: Dempster, *Exploring*, 112–19.

21. Septuagint studies have flowered in recent years: see Jobes and Silva, *Invitation*. "LXX" (Roman numerals for "seventy") abbreviates it due to a legend that seventy scholars produced identical translations in seventy days.

22. These three are codices, i.e., bound books with spines, like modern books,

to date the reordering of the Old Testament books there. Nevertheless, the order is closer to the one Christians now maintain than to that of the Hebrew Bible, so the Septuagint is the basis of the order now standard among Christians.[23] Until the second century AD books were kept as scrolls, stored in no order, not bound books reflecting the established order. The variation from the Hebrew order is likely due to limited Christian contact with the Jewish community "because relations with the Jews were often unhappy"[24] meaning that knowledge of the Jewish order of the books faded.

In Jerome's Latin Vulgate (AD 405) the order of the Old Testament books with which Christians are familiar was standardized.[25] The Latin Vulgate eventually displaced the Septuagint and the earlier Latin versions and became the standard Christian Bible for the next 1,000 years. This permanently established the order of the books of the Old Testament with which all Christians are now familiar.[26]

JESUS AND THE NEW TESTAMENT AUTHORS ENDORSED TANAK

Like people who remember phones that hung on the wall, Jesus and the New Testament authors knew and used the original Tanak structure before the Christian order came to be. This is clear in many ways. A century ago, William Henry Green wrote that Jesus and the New Testament authors gave their "sanction to the canon as it existed among the Jews" "both negatively and positively."[27] Negatively, while they accused their Jewish contemporaries

rather than scrolls. The codex replaced the scroll beginning in the second century AD. They are *Codex Sinaiticus* (fourth cent. AD), *Codex Vaticanus* (fourth cent.), and *Codex Alexandrinus* (fifth cent.). For the contents and order of the various books, see Bruce, *Canon*, 69. Note also that these codices included varying portions of the Apocrypha.

23. See Bruce, *Canon*, 47. We do have lists of the Old Testament books, provided by Christian writers, which pre-date the Septuagint. These lists also vary in their order of the books, but they are closer to the current order Christians use than to that of the Hebrew Bible, showing that the rearrangement dates to at least the late second century AD. See Bruce, *Canon*, 70–76 for the lists of Melito, Bishop of Sardis (ca. AD 170) and Origen (AD 185–254).

24. See Beckwith, *OT Canon*, 390–91.

25. Jerome's Vulgate included the Apocryphal books, by order of the Pope who commissioned the translation.

26. The Roman Catholic Old Testament contains the apocrypha, and the Orthodox Churches also include a (somewhat varied) set of apocrypha books. The Orthodox Churches have always used the Septuagint as their Old Testament, but the order (of the non-apocryphal books) is the same as the Latin Vulgate and Christian Bibles.

27. Green, *Introduction*, 141.

of misinterpreting the Scriptures, "they never charge them with mutilating or corrupting the word of God" by their view of the canon.[28] As Green writes, Jesus "could not have passed it over in silence if they had been guilty of excluding whole books from the canon which properly belonged there, or inserting that which was not really inspired by God."[29]

Positive endorsement of the Jewish canon in the New Testament takes several forms.[30] There are explicit statements. For example, Paul wrote, "the Jews were entrusted with the oracles of God" (Romans 3:2). When Paul wrote, "All Scripture is breathed out by God" (2 Timothy 3:16), his primary reference is to the Old Testament and since he elaborates no further, it is clear that he has in mind the "Scriptures" upon which the Jewish community agreed. His declaration that "all" Scripture is God's word validates the entire Hebrew Bible as inspired by God. A second form of endorsement is in the abundant references to Scripture as a whole, or its units, by their traditional Jewish designations. This affirms them as God's words and, thus, as reliable and authoritative. Examples would include John 10:25, Matthew 5:17 and Romans 3:21. Green summarizes, "To those who reverently accept the authority of Christ and his apostles, the sanction thus given to the canon of the Jews is the highest possible proof if its correctness."[31]

So, Jesus and the New Testament authors endorsed the Jewish canon of Scripture. Further, they referred to it exactly as did their Jewish contemporaries. They sometimes refer to the entire Hebrew Bible as "the holy Scriptures" (Romans 1:2), "The Law" (Romans 3:19, summarizing 3:10–18), "the Prophets" (Luke 24:25), etc.[32] Other times, as the Jews did, they refer to the Hebrew Bible by a two-part designation, such as "the law and the prophets" (e.g., Matthew 5:17), etc.[33] Finally, the New Testament refers to the Hebrew Bible by a three-part designation (Luke 24:44, "the Law of Moses and the Prophets and the Psalms" [Psalms begins the Writings]). We will see below that looking at the Hebrew Bible as Tanak opens fresh understanding of the Hebrew Bible that the later Christian rearrangement obscures.

28. Green, *Canon*, 141. Note that the word "canon" is a Christian term that comes into use later; it is used here for convenience.

29. Green, *Canon*, 141.

30. See Green, *Canon*, 141–44.

31. Green, *Canon*, 144.

32. For a comprehensive list see Beckwith, *Canon*, 105–9.

33. Dempster, *Exploring*, 106.

What we Know about the Order of the Books in Tanak

We have shown that Jesus and the New Testament authors endorsed the Tanak structure of the Hebrew Bible. But are we rock-solid certain of the order of the books in the three sections of Tanak? Broadly we can say these things.[34] There has never been any question about the order of the books in the Torah; they have always been ordered (in Hebrew and Christian Bibles) as Genesis, Exodus, Leviticus, Numbers, and Deuteronomy, their chronological order. There has been near unanimity about the order of the Former Prophets, the order being Joshua, Judges, Samuel and Kings, which also occur in chronological order. There has been considerable diversity regarding the order of the Latter Prophets, Isaiah, Jeremiah, Ezekiel and the Twelve being the typical order. There has been substantial variation in the order of the books in the Writings, but little variation in how they begin and end. The Hebrew Bible as it has come down to us begins with Psalms and ends with Chronicles. What can we say about the order of the books in the Writings in Jesus' day?

Does Luke 24 Establish the Order of the Writings?[35]

There are two New Testament passages that deserve attention regarding this question. The first is Luke 24:44, where Jesus speaks to his disciples on the Emmaus Road saying, "These are my words that I spoke to you while I was still with you, that everything written about me in the Law of Moses and the Prophets and the Psalms must be fulfilled." Many have taken "Psalms" as a reference to the third unit of Tanak, the Writings, referred to by the first book in the unit.[36] If so, this shows that the order of the Writings in Jesus day was the same as it has come down to us. Others point out that "Psalms" could mean simply "the book of Psalms," specified from the Writings because it is a book uniquely filled with messianic material,[37] which would mean that it says nothing about the order of the Writings in Jesus' day. In that case, it still shows knowledge and endorsement of the three-part division of Tanak, though it communicates nothing about the specific order of the third unit, the Writings. While both views have defenders, the evidence strongly favors understanding "Psalms" as standing for the first book of the

34. For detailed analysis see Beckwith, *OT Canon*, 449–71.

35. The third Tanak unit comes to be called "the Writings" by the Rabbis later. The term is used here for convenience.

36. For example, Bock, *Luke*, 621; Dempster, *Exploring*, 120–21.

37. Dodd pointed this out in *According to the Scriptures.*

Writings.[38] This means that in Jesus' day, the Writings began with Psalms, just as they do in the Hebrew Bible as it has come down to us.

Does Matthew 23:35 Establish the Order of the Writings?

The other text that requires discussion is Matthew 23:33–35 (= Luke 11:51). Jesus says, "You serpents, you brood of vipers, how are you to escape being sentenced to hell? Therefore I send you prophets and wise men and scribes, some of whom you will kill and crucify and some you will flog in your synagogues and persecute from town to town, so that on you may come all the righteous blood shed on earth, from the blood of innocent Abel to the blood of Zechariah the son of Barachiah, whom you murdered between the sanctuary and the altar."

This text has been widely understood to refer to the first and the last murders in Scripture, as arranged in Tanak. That is, Abel's murder is recorded in the first book of Tanak (Genesis 4:8), while the last murder is recorded in 2 Chronicles 24:20–22, in the last book of Tanak. This would mean that the Writings in Jesus' day ended with Chronicles, just as it has come down to us. This is, indeed, the best understanding of the text. As France explains, "because it is recorded toward the end of 2 Chronicles, the last book of the Hebrew canon, it suitably rounds off the biblical record of God's servants killed for their loyalty."[39] Jesus is saying, "from the beginning of Scripture to its end."

There is a difficult matter for biblical scholarship in general in this text, though not for the issue we are discussing.[40] The parallel passage, Luke 11:51, quite clearly shows that the "Zechariah" Jesus has in mind is the son of Jehoiada, since Luke repeats the word "require" drawn from 2 Chronicles 24:22. Thus, in spite of the difficulty attending the passage, it is quite clear that the martyr here is the one from 2 Chronicles 24:20–22, as most scholars

38. See Bock, *Luke*, 1917–37.

39. France, *Matthew*, 880.

40. The difficulty is that while Matthew records Jesus as saying that Zechariah was "the son of Berechiah," 2 Chronicles 24:20 names him "Zechariah, son of Jehoiada." This is the basis of Green's statement that the identity of this "Zechariah" is in doubt. Various solutions have been proposed for this seeming contradiction, from holding that Jesus or Matthew made a mistake, to arguing that a copyist error occurred early in the history of copying the manuscripts. Wenham, *Christ*, 77–81, lays out eight possible approaches. The most satisfying seems to be that Zechariah was the *son* of Berachiah and the *grandson* of Jehoiada, since the Hebrew word for "son" and "grandson" is the same word. This would mean that both Jesus (who drew upon common knowledge in his time that has been lost) and 2 Chronicles were correct, and Wenham demonstrates this explanation is quite plausible.

have always held and thus is the last martyr mentioned in the last book in the Hebrew order of Tanak. So, this text clearly demonstrates that in Jesus' day, the Writings ended with Chronicles, just as does the contemporary Hebrew Bible.

Our examination of Luke 24:44 and Matthew 23:35 has shown that, despite variation in the order of the other books in the Writings, the Writings began with Psalms and ended with Chronicles in Jesus' day, just as the Hebrew Bible has come down to us.

THE TANAK ORDER MAKES A DIFFERENCE

We have shown that the Hebrew Bible is arranged as Tanak, listed the order of the books in each section of Tanak, and shown that Jesus and the New Testament authors endorsed the Tanak arrangement. But this raises an important question: does it make any difference which order readers use? There are reasons to answer "yes."

One reason is that, like the chapters in a novel or the episodes in a film, the order in which things are presented makes a difference.[41] Another reason is more concrete: the proof is in the pudding. In other words, if we find examples where order seems to make a difference, then the point is made. Many examples might be cited. The fact that Genesis 11:1–9, describing a time when there was a unified human language, *follows* Genesis 10, which lists many human languages (it is a flashback) changes the way we read Genesis 11. It injects a sense of wonder that those who rebelled against God in chapter 11 could have imagined that they could succeed. Or again, the placing of Genesis 38 just before Genesis 39 affects how we read Genesis 39. Commentators observe that Genesis 38, the story of Judah and Tamar, seems to interrupt the story of Joseph that has just begun in 37:2.[42] Why is a story about Judah introduced here? One clear reason is that by reading about Judah's poor integrity and sexual misconduct in chapter 38, the author shines a spotlight on the opposite traits that Joseph displays in Genesis 39, when he is tempted by Potipher's wife. So, biblical authors use the ordering of stories for artistic effect.

41. Sailhamer dubs this "con-textuality," which he defines for biblical study as, "the effect on meaning of the relative position of a biblical book within a prescribed order of reading" (*Introduction* 213; see 213–15; 249–52). Put more simply, "context influences meaning," and film makers call this "montage" (*Introduction*, 214).

42. For example, the usually perceptive Brueggemann (*Genesis*, 308) says of Genesis 38, "This peculiar chapter stands alone, without connection to the context. It is isolated in every way and is most enigmatic."

John Sailhamer illustrates the importance of the order of the biblical books in Tanak. He observes that Ruth "follows the book of Judges in the English Bible, whereas in the Hebrew Bible it follows the book of Proverbs."[43] Proverbs ends (31:10–31) describing the "*virtuous woman*" (31:10), whose "deeds will praise her *in the gates*" (31:31). It is no coincidence that Boaz says of Ruth, "All those *in the gate* of my people know that you are a *virtuous woman*" (Ruth 3:11)! By ordering the books in this way, the author shows that the common perception that Ruth is a rather irrelevant add-on to Hebrew Scripture is a misperception. The author of Tanak intended the book as an illustration of the wisdom theme of the godly female. By casting a Gentile in this role, he also highlights the Torah teaching that God's kingdom was always intended to embrace many beyond Israel. The entire Hebrew Bible seems to illustrate this.[44] We therefore conclude that reading the Hebrew Bible in the Tanak order makes a difference.

CONCLUSION: CHRISTIANS SHOULD READ THE OLD TESTAMENT AS JESUS DID

Jesus and the authors of the New Testament endorsed the Tanak structure of the Hebrew Bible. Although the order of the books in the Prophets and the Writings can be debated, the best evidence is that the units began and ended in Jesus' day as they do in the current Hebrew Bible.

Since Jesus endorsed the Tanak structure, it makes sense to suggest that Christians read it as Jesus did. If the Tanak arrangement was intentional, considerable weight accrues to the suggestion. Finally, if there is evidence that the Tanak order was intended to guide the audience in detecting central themes, continuities, and lessons, then that suggestion becomes an imperative. The next chapter will address these issues.

43. Sailhamer, *Introduction*, 213.

44. DeRouchie, *Understand*, 326–29.

Chapter 4

Tanak is Intended to Show the Primacy of the Torah

We all know that well-told stories move toward a goal. The *Star Wars* episodes all move toward the goal of the destruction of the reign of the dark side. Israel's story in the Torah moves toward the goal of entering the promised land. Everyone's life is a story moving toward a goal. The philosopher Kierkegaard correctly said that "Life can only be understood backwards; but it must be lived forwards." But *how in the world* can we have that twenty-twenty hindsight to understand life before we live it? Well, *from this world*, we cannot. But in the Tanak, God has divulged the lessons that become clear from living life. He has disclosed what hindsight will eventually unveil so that we can live life forwards while understanding it backwards, but without having to learn it all by experience! Tanak's structure announces that the Torah is the treasure-chest of those lessons. Reading the Torah is to step into the brilliant sunlight of God's wisdom.

Of course, there are many things we will not and do not need to know. Deuteronomy 29:29 insists that "The secret things belong to the LORD our God, but the things that are revealed belong to us and to our children forever, that we may do all the words of this law." Tanak's purpose is to steer us to the Torah as the gold-mine of hindsight written as foresight. The Torah's foresight is intended to minimize having to learn from hindsight. Reading the Torah is the best way to minimize how often we repeat John Greenleaf

Whittier's lament: "Of all the words of mice and men, the saddest are, 'It might have been.'" A prime lesson: "obey God's instruction."

TANAK WAS INTENTIONAL

To sustain these allegations about the purpose of the Tanak arrangement, we must first show that the arrangement was intentional. Several considerations affirm this. The first evidence of intentionality is that the arrangement was not arbitrary. While certain sections are clearly chronological others are clearly not. Some larger plan was therefore at work. A second factor is similar: the Tanak arrangement is not intuitive. The Tanak form was chosen rather than some other choices, such as chronological or topical arrangement. We have already suggested a plausible organizational principle derived from Jeremiah (18:18) and Ezekiel (7:26), who saw three sorts of revelation by God: law, prophecy, and wise counsel.[1] It is reasonable to see these three categories as the seed from which the three-branched Tanak tree grew. Law is in the Torah, prophecy in the Prophets, and wise counsel in the Writings. Let us develop this suggestion.

The concept of Scripture begins with the Torah. McDonald observes, "In a very real sense, Israel had a canon when the tradition of Moses receiving the Torah on Sinai was accepted into the community."[2] The concept of prophecy as a form of revelation arises when Moses, regarded as *the* prophet (Deut 34:10), tells Israel, "The LORD said . . . I will raise up for them a prophet like you" (Deut 18:17–18). Dempster well observes, "This points ahead to the next collection of Scripture, in which prophets will be emphasized—prophets who are made in the Mosaic image but do not measure up to his lofty status."[3]

The third evidence is less obvious. The words of Jeremiah 18:18 and Ezekiel 7:26 testify to their belief in revelation from God that is distinct from law and prophets. Both Jeremiah and Ezekiel speak of "counsel" (using the same Hebrew word). Is it only a coincidence that the same Hebrew term appears at the head of the Writings in Psalm 1:1, "Blessed is the one who does not walk in the *counsel* of the wicked"? This suggests that the Writings are intended as godly "counsel" from the wise.

1. Dempster, *Exploring*, 92; he is following Margolis, *Hebrew Scriptures*.

2. McDonald, *Canon*, 20. "Canon" refers to a set of books considered authoritative, such as the Bible.

3. Dempster, *Exploring*, 93. That the prophetic gift ceased after Malachi was widely acknowledged among the Jews, e.g., 1 Maccabees 9:26–27; Josephus, *Against Apion*, 1:7–8.

The evidence is persuasive that the Tanak arrangement was intentional. Since it was intentional, we would expect the author to leave clues for the audience about why he chose this structure. In fact, the clues are there! They show that the Torah is God's foundational message. The Law is to the Prophets and the Writings as an acorn is to a tree, a topic sentences is to a paragraph, a motif is to a musical composition: it gives birth to the rest. That makes the Prophets and the Writings inspired elaboration and commentary on the Torah, as the Jewish community has always held. But before we examine the clues, we must discuss the authorship of Tanak.

THE AUTHORSHIP OF TANAK

Until modern times, Christians had a straightforward, biblically informed, if rather simple, approach to the authorship and date of the books in the Hebrew Bible. They took the Bible at face value and examined what it revealed about the origins of the Scriptures. The primary conclusion was that Jesus accepted the Hebrew Bible as the Word of God and they accepted that as final. Thus, what the Old Testament books revealed about their authorship was considered the Word of God on the subject. Evidence within Scripture ("internal evidence"), such as people or events mentioned, was mined so that dates of composition for individual books could be determined or approximated. It also seemed clear from Jesus and the New Testament authors that Moses wrote the Torah and that his life could be dated to around 1400 BC. Scholars were aware of more data, such as the writings of Josephus (about AD 37 to 100) and the Jewish rabbis ("external evidence"), but it was generally consistent with what Scripture suggested.

This situation began to change in 1753 when a French physician named Jean Astruc published a book that suggested a more complex history behind the writing of the Hebrew Bible. He based his new theory upon observations he made from reading Scripture. For example, he noticed that in Genesis (in Hebrew) God was called by two different names, *elohim* ("God") and YHWH (God's personal name).[4] He also noticed that there were three

4. God's name in Hebrew is spelled "Yahweh." It is derived from the verb "to be" and translated "I am who I am" (Exod 3:14). Since Hebrew was written without vowels, it is actually "YHWH." The Jews decided early (before 250 BC) to prevent anyone misusing God's name by never allowing anyone to pronounce it! To clue public readers of Scripture to this they wrote the vowels to another word for God ("Lord") around the Hebrew consonants of God's name; since the vowels didn't match the consonants, the readers was reminded to say "Adonai" ("Lord") out loud in reading, pronouncing what the vowels would mean. (This reading convention is called a *kethiv-qere*.) The earliest translator of the Pentateuch from Hebrew into English was the skilled linguist William

stories in Genesis in which someone lied about his wife being his sister (Gen 12:13, 20:2, 26:7). Astruc was a pious man and was reluctant to raise such questions. Nevertheless, he theorized that Genesis and the Pentateuch contained such oddities because there was a more complicated history behind the writing of the Pentateuch than previously believed. Perhaps there had been several documents, written centuries apart, containing variations on the same stories, much like stories change when whispered from person to person around a campfire. He suggested that the different names for God reflected different periods in Israel's history, eventually combined in our Bible as if they were current at the same time. Thus, when we read Genesis, we encounter a composite book put together from the earlier sources, in which the author included all the traditions he knew about. Astruc's theory circulated widely and with time gained a large following. Others began noticing more elements in the text of the Pentateuch that were also hard to explain. For example, in Genesis 14:14 Abraham is said to have pursued those who kidnapped his relative Lot "to Dan." But that territory was not named "Dan" until after Moses' death. Numerous scholars concluded from this that the Pentateuch could not have been written by Moses; it must have been written later. This theory was eventually christened the "documentary hypothesis."[5] Some were attracted to the theory because they were skeptical about Scripture anyway and this provided them reason to deconstruct Christian belief. Others were puzzled by the issues that came to light in these discussions and acknowledged that honesty demanded explanation for these issues. The general consensus in the twenty-first-century among (often skeptical) scholars is that a version of the documentary hypothesis is the place to begin study of the Hebrew Bible.[6] The most common form of the theory proposes that there must have been four documents that served as the basis for the Pentateuch, named "J," "E," "D," and "P."[7] Long-opposed

Tyndale (1530). But he did not know this convention, so he spelled into English what he saw on the page, and thus invented a non-existent name for God, "Jehovah." The King James Version (1611) translators still did not understand this convention and so replicated the mistake in their translation, which injected it into the English-speaking world. Most modern translations honor the traditional Jewish practice by rendering God's name as "LORD" (all caps, but smaller caps for "ORD"); when the Hebrew says "Adonai," translators render it "Lord."

5. For a statement and critique see Kaiser, *Documents*, 53–54, 133–38.

6. See, for example, Coogan and Chapman, *Old Testament*, 45–54, esp. 47.

7. "J" is for the document that used "Jehovah" ("Yahweh" is now known to be more accurate) as God's name (written 950 BC); "E" is for the later document (850 BC) that used the Hebrew term *elohim* ("God") to refer to God; "D" represents the "Deuteronomist" (630 BC), who wrote Deuteronomy, and "P" is for the "Priestly" document (550 BC), which fixated on sacrifice, temple worship, and other priestly interests. "P"

by conservative scholars, the theory has recently been criticized outside those circles.[8]

Generally speaking, those who believe the Bible to be God's Word have been reticent to fully embrace the documentary hypothesis, since the typical statement of the theory dismisses or substantially modifies the traditional concept of biblical inspiration and holds a low regard for the reliability of the Bible in general. However, the issues that gave rise to the theory must be addressed. While detailed analysis of these issues is beyond the scope of this book, two observations are appropriate here. The first is that there is a large literature that addresses the numerous legitimate questions that discussions of the documentary hypothesis have raised.[9] The second observation is that the approach adopted here to the authorship of Tanak helps to address many of these issues.

Jesus and the New Testament authors seem clearly to affirm that Moses wrote the Torah,[10] so that is assumed here. But what shall we say about "late" words in the text like, "he pursued them to Dan" in Gen 14:14? The view advocated here is that Moses wrote the bulk of the Torah and that the Torah as it now stands is substantially as he wrote it. However, the author who put Tanak into its present form, or other prophets, did editorial work on the text, under the inspiration of the Holy Spirit.[11] Since that author did this work before the time of Jesus and Jesus endorsed the Tanak as we now have it, Christians receive the editor's work as inspired. The author of Tanak arranged the inspired books into the Law, the Prophets, and the Writings. He also arranged the books within each category into the order they now

---

combined these four sources into the current Pentateuch (Coogan, *Old Testament*, 52–53). The documents are not known to have existed, but the theory proposes that they must have existed.

8. See Coogan, *Old Testament*, 52–53; Representative of recent attacks, see Whybray, *Pentateuch* and Wiseman, *Ancient Records*. Representing conservative rebuttals see Harrison, *Introduction*, 3–61.

9. All the original issues that Astruc raised are now recognized as mistakes on our part, due to our shallow knowledge of the ancient Near East ("ANE"). For example, it seemed to Astruc, and to many after him, that two names for a deity at the same time was odd. However, we now know that this was a routine feature of many ANE cultures. See, e.g., the work of Egyptologist Kenneth Kitchen, *Ancient Orient*, 112–26; and Kitchen, *Reliability*.

10. Mosaic authorship of the Pentateuch was undisputed before 1753. On the history see Alexander, "Authorship," 61–72. The view before the Enlightenment was based upon numerous OT (e.g., Exodus 17:14, 34:27; Joshua 1:8, etc.) and NT references (e.g., Matthew 19:8; March 12:26; John 5:46–47; Romans 10:5, etc.).

11. For an elaboration and defense of the position adopted here, see Merrill et al., *Word and World*, 79–92; also Sailhamer, *Introduction*, 239–52; Sailhamer, *Meaning*, 48–56; Dempster, *Dominion and Dynasty*, 37–41; Block, *Deuteronomy*, 29–33.

occupy. Further, he added material at the transition points between the Law and the Prophets and between the Prophets and the Writings. These transitions guide the reader[12] in understanding how to read the sections. He also added brief material at the end of each section (Law, Prophets, Writings) to guide the reader. Finally, he is the likely source of other elements of the text that stand out to us.[13]

The assumption of editorial work by the author of Tanak provides a straightforward explanation of "late" elements in the text. He would be the one who updated some ancient wordings so that the later audience could better understand the text, such as the anachronistic "Dan" of Genesis 14:14. Scholars have widely acknowledged that such updating *must* have occurred, since it is right there in the text. But attributing this to the author of Tanak who put Tanak in its final form provides a plausible understanding of who the updater was.[14] He also would have added other features that reflect a time after Moses, such as Moses' death notice (Deut 34:5–9), and the observation that "there has not arisen a prophet since in Israel like Moses" (Deut 34:10). This observation had to be written after prophecy had ceased so that the conclusion would be accurate (that is, the fifth century BC).[15] We *know* that someone had to arrange Tanak as it has stood since before Jesus'

12. To be precise, the Bible was written in an oral culture, and thus was written to be read out loud since few people could read. Authors wrote to be *heard* by the audience, though today they serve the same function for the reader. On orality, see Harvey, *Listening*; Alter, *Art*; Bar-Efrat, *Narrative Art*.

13. "The study of the history of Hebrew literature . . . is a different enterprise from studying the form and function of the Pentateuch in the shape accorded it by the community of faith as its canonical scriptures" (Childs, *Introduction*, 128). We prefer "studying the form and function of the Pentateuch in the shape accorded to it by the final inspired prophet and accepted by Jesus [as] canonical scriptures" (Childs, *Introduction*, 128).

14. This view is better than proposing that late words must signal a late book. Two issues must be explained: the evidence that Torah elements are "early" and the evidence of "late" material. The proposal here accounts for both, whereas the "late" view has more trouble explaining the early elements, and often does so by simply dispensing with the biblical claims. We have very substantial reasons to believe not only that Moses wrote the Torah, but that he wrote it when the Jews and Christians long held that he did, in the mid-second millennium BC, about 1400 BC. Recent evidence (since 1906) of the Hittite treaty forms called "Suzerain-Vassal" treaties is significant evidence for the traditional date. See Kitchen, *Reliability*, 492–3; Craigie, *Deuteronomy*, 20–29; Merrill, *Deuteronomy*, 22–23. The most recent scholarship shows the parallels with Hittite treaties are stronger than with later treaties.

15. Some have dated certain Hebrew Bible books later than the traditional views did because they contain predictive prophecy that turned out to be accurate, and not believing that is possible, they choose to date them late, after the events had occurred. Those who believe God can inspire predictive prophecy have no need to postdate the books due to that feature.

time and that Jesus approved that form as inspired Scripture, validating the author's additions. We therefore propose that late words in the text, later additions to what the original author wrote and other features that required a later hand,[16] came from the author of Tanak.[17] This view explains both the "early" and the "late" material in the Torah without having to disagree with Jesus about Moses' authorship.

TANAK WAS INTENDED TO SHOW THE PRIMACY OF THE TORAH

The Jews Hold to the Primacy of the Torah

The initial evidence that Tanak was arranged to establish the Torah's primacy is the long-held Jewish support for this view. If Einstein speaks about relativity, we listen because he developed the theory. Likewise, when the Jewish community speaks about their book, attending to their view is fitting. Their belief is evidence of what sustained engagement with Tanak yields.

The Jewish exaltation of the Torah is common knowledge. Prominent Jewish author Jacob Neusner says of the Torah, "the first five books, Genesis through Deuteronomy, called the 'Law of Moses' [is] regarded as the heart of the Tanakh."[18] Beckwith writes, "the rabbis attributed a higher degree of sanctity to the Pentateuch, as being the earliest and most important section of the canon."[19] Christians eventually lost this perspective, but Judaism never did.

16. This might help explain a writing style that seems to differ from that of the author of a book, as do other factors such as authors transcribing material from sources, thereby incorporating a style that varies from the author's.

17. We do not know who did this. Ezra, Nehemiah, and Judas Maccabeus have been suggested. Since the earliest evidence we have for Tanak outside Scripture is in the second (or third) century BC, it cannot be later than that.

18. Neusner, "Torah," 637. Neusner reflects the perspective declared 2,000 years ago in the Mishnah, the sayings of the rabbis from about 200 BC to AD 200 that were committed to writing about AD 200. The Law takes priority in the Mishnah. For example, in the Mishnah, tractate ("book") *Aboth* ("The Fathers"), we read, "Great is the Law which bestows life upon those that practice it in this world and in the world to come" (*Aboth* 6:7). Blackman, Mishnah, *Aboth* is in volume 4. See also *Aboth* 1:13, 3:2, 6:2, 6:10.

19. Beckwith, *OT Canon*, 143.

General Recognition that the Prophets and Writings Restate the Torah

An old Arabian proverb says, He who knows and knows that he knows, listen to him! Scholars have long known that the Prophets and the Writings repeat the Torah message. For example, Fee and Stuart explain, "*The prophets' message is not original.* The prophets were inspired by God to present to their generation the essential content of the original Mosaic covenant's warnings and promises (cursings and blessings). Therefore, when we read the prophets' words, what we read is . . . the same message in essence delivered by God originally through Moses."[20]

Waltke makes a similar observation about the Psalms, which introduce the Writings. Speaking of the five-part structure of the Psalter, Waltke says, "Jewish tradition explains this second 'Pentateuch' as a conscious echo of the first," and then concludes, "Moses instituted Israel's liturgical elements. . . . David, Israel's Mozart, transformed the Mosaic liturgy into opera by putting it on the stage of the temple and by accompanying it with the music and libretto of his psalms."[21] The Prophets and Writings are not stuttering, but they are repeating Moses' message.

Structural Clues in Tanak to the Primacy of the Torah: The Introductions

Like a good mystery writer, the author of Tanak left clues to guide the reader to the proper conclusion. The Prophets open with Joshua, and Joshua opens this way (Joshua 1:8): "This Book of the Law shall not depart from your mouth, but you shall meditate on it day and night, so that you may be careful to do according to all that is written in it. For then you will make your way prosperous and then you will have good success." The word translated "law" is *torah* and it is referred to as a "book of the Torah." Since Deut 31:23–27, which refers to the same events as Joshua 1, states, "When Moses had finished writing the words of this *torah* in a book to the very end" (31:24), *torah* here refers to the text of Genesis to Deuteronomy.[22] So, the Prophets

20. Fee and Stuart, *How to Read*, 193–94, emphasis in original. Waltke makes a similar affirmation in Waltke, *Theology*, 805: "The prophets interpret Israel's history, explaining its failures as due to her covenant infidelity."

21. Waltke, *Theology*, 884.

22. Scholars often limit this "book of the law" to Deuteronomy or a portion of it, e.g., Block, *Deuteronomy*, 27–33. Many others see it as the Pentateuch, e.g., Ross, *Psalms*, 1:188–89; Sailhamer, *Meaning*, 23, 28, 52–54; Dempster, *Dominion and Dynasty*, 129; Childs, *Introduction*, 244–47, who builds a strong case that while Deuteronomy is the

open with an exhortation to "meditate on *torah* day and night" (Joshua 1:8). There is also a promise about what results from such meditation (Joshua 1:8): "prosperity" (*tslach*) and "success" (*sacal*). These results are precisely what the Torah promised, since the Torah states that those who disobey the Mosaic laws "will not prosper" (*tslach*) (Deut 28:29) and that those who "keep the words of this covenant and do them" will "prosper/be successful" (*sacal*) (Deut 29:9). Joshua thus begins the Prophets with a one-sentence summary of the argument of the Torah: obey the Torah and you will prosper! Joshua does not open pointing the reader fundamentally forward, to brand new revelation, but backward, to Torah observance and the Torah's promised rewards. This implies that the Torah is the foundation, while the Prophets are superstructure built upon that foundation. Wenham agrees: "The message of the book of Joshua seems to be that Israel was careful by and large to fulfill its covenant obligations and that this is why it enjoyed the blessings conditional on obedience and was able to conquer the land."[23] Joshua is superstructure built upon the foundation of the Torah: its purpose is to demonstrate that the argument of the Torah proved true in Joshua's generation. It is inspired Scripture, but its purpose is to validate the Torah! That the author of Tanak places this imperative at the opening of Joshua ("meditate on Torah day and night") strongly suggests that the purpose of the Prophets as a whole is what Joshua argues at their beginning: obey the Torah and you will prosper. The same lesson is certainly taught in Judges, the next book in the Prophets, except that it is taught in the negative. The last sentence in Judges is, "In those days Israel had no king; everyone did what was right in his own eyes" (21:25). The message is that because Israel did not obey God as their king, they had descended into corruption and

part of the Torah most often cited and alluded to, "the constant reference to sacred events which are not mentioned in Deuteronomy confirms the view that the law as encompassed in the entire Pentateuch is assumed" (247). Two considerations support the meaning "Pentateuch." If Moses wrote the bulk of the Pentateuch, then Deut 31:24 is the *only* statement saying that "Moses finished writing the words of this *torah* in a book to the very end," and as this statement is quite near the end of Deuteronomy, and Moses' life, when else would he have written it? Second, as Tanak was arranged in the form in which it has come down to us by an editor after Moses' time, it is quite reasonable that *he* used the word "*torah*" as the Jews had come to use it by the time he did his work (likely in the mid-second century, BC), as the term for the Pentateuch. To read it in the more limited sense is to ignore the intentional arrangement of the Hebrew Bible in its final form, in which the Prophets and the Writings follow the Torah. As Bruce wrote, "Similar considerations apply to almost every part of the Old Testament. We have to ask what each part meant in its original form and setting, what it meant when it was embodied in a larger *corpus*, and what it meant in the completed Hebrew Bible" (Bruce, *Canon*, 324).

23. Wenham, "Deuteronomic Theology," 146–7.

anarchy, the opposite of prospering.[24] That the first two books in the Prophets argue what Joshua 1:8 says is strong evidence that the purpose of the Prophets as a whole is validating the Torah's argument.

That the purpose of the Prophets is to elaborate upon the Torah is validated again in the Former Prophets: Joshua, Judges, Samuel and Kings. First, these books demonstrate in the history of Israel the truth of the Torah predictions about Israel's fate. That Israel would fail as a nation is foreshadowed in the story of Adam and Eve's expulsion from the Garden (Genesis 3:1–7, 8–24) and the story of Moses' exclusion from Canaan. (Numbers 20:1–12).[25] But more obviously the dispersion of Israel among the nations was prophesied by Moses in Deuteronomy 29:22–30:10; 31:19–29. The Former Prophets in their entirety thus expound in detail the historical outworking of Moses' Torah prediction.

It is striking that the Writings begin exactly as did the Prophets! Psalm 1:1–3 says, "Blessed is the man who[se]. . . . delight is in the law of the LORD and on his law he meditates day and night. He is like a tree planted by streams of water that yields its fruit in its season and its leaf does not wither. In all that he does, he prospers." The vocabulary about to the Torah parallels Joshua 1:8 and so does the reward: he "prospers" (*tsalach*) (Psalm 1:3) and succeeds (*sacal*) (Psalm 2:10).[26]

If someone says, "It's like déjà vu all over again," "It's like déjà vu all over again," we recognize that the exact repetition is exactly intentional! It therefore seems certain that the author of Tanak arranged Psalms 1 and 2 to head the Psalms so that the opening of the Writings would parallel the opening of the Prophets.[27] In the Christian arrangement of Old Testament, the parallel wording of Joshua 1 and Psalm 1 might be noticed but its function of introducing the other two major units of Scripture after the Torah is lost! Only by approaching the Hebrew Bible in the Tanak order can this

24. Judges 21:25 (see 17:6, 18:1, 19:1) has a double meaning: a human king and God as Israel's king.

25. Waltke, *Theology*, 150.

26. The ESV translates the term "be wise." Psalms 1 and 2 serve as the Psalter introduction (Mays, *Psalms*, 15; Waltke, *Theology*, 884). This Hebrew word for "bless" frames Psalms 1 and 2, binding these two together as a unit introducing the Psalms: Waltke, *Theology*, 884, n. 56. See Waltke, *Theology*, 884, n. 56 for more commonalities.

27. It is to be noted that Psalms 1 and 2, which introduce the Psalter, are both without a superscription, as Psalms 3–9 all have. Did the author of Tanak compose Psalms 1 and 2 to suit his purpose, or did he simply place these anonymous psalms at the front due to their wording? We do not know. But the fact that they repeat the exhortation and the rewards from Joshua 1 using the same vocabulary suggests one of these. It seems most likely that God's charge to Joshua as it now stands was included in Joshua and that the repetition in Psalms 1–2 is the work of the Tanak author.

parallel be fully appreciated. The parallel introductions to the Prophets and the Writings urges the conclusion that the author of Tanak has the same purpose in mind in using it in both places. He wants to clue the reader in that he is arguing that success depends upon "meditating on Torah day and night."

But here an important distinction should be noticed. The context of the two exhortation to meditate on the Torah differs. The context in Joshua suggests that the result of continual Torah meditation is success for the nation. Success here relates to what Dempster calls "dominion and dynasty,"[28] i.e., conquering the land of Canaan and the development of the dynasty of kings that will rule it. The reward is corporate success. The content of the Former and Latter Prophets is certainly consistent with this vision of the purpose of the Prophets.

The context of the same exhortation in the Psalms suggests a different purpose in the Writings: wisdom. The Hebrew term (*hochma*) means "skillful living," the good judgment to obey the Torah in daily circumstances. The reward for meditation on the Torah is "prospering" (Psalm 1:3), i.e., "happiness,"[29] for the individual (Psalm 1:2) and the nations (2:12). Psalm 1 suggests that the wisdom obtained by Torah meditation (1:1–3) will bring individual happiness and blessing from God (1:1, 6). But in Psalm 2 the reward is happiness (2:10 in Hebrew; 2:12) for the godly in an ungodly world (2:1–3) and national happiness if nations will bow to God (2:8–12). The Writings fit this description. We conclude that the Prophets and the Writings both begin by summarizing the message they were composed to convey: obey the Torah and you will prosper! The means: mediation on the Torah day and night (Joshua 1:8; Psalm 1:1–3).

Structural Clues in Tanak to the Primacy of the Torah: The Conclusions

The author of Tanak repeats himself when he ends each unit! Malachi concludes the Prophets saying (4:4), "Remember the law [*torah*] of my servant Moses, the statutes and rules that I commanded him at Horeb." Malachi's final exhortation summarizes his book. Alden states, "This verse, in a sense, closes the entire book. Malachi began with an illustration from Genesis (Jacob and Esau) and spent most of the first half of the book reminding priests

28. Dempster, *Dominion and Dynasty* (2003).

29. The Hebrew word used here, often translated "blessed," communicates that the blessing is "happiness."

and people of the need to keep the Mosaic Law."[30] As an exhortation to obey the Torah, it ends the Prophets as they began in Joshua 1: obey the Torah and you will succeed! It's like déjà vu all over again.

Chronicles ends the Writings similarly. The *torah* ("Book of the Law," etc.) is mentioned fourteen times in chapters 34 and 35 alone. Near the end is a description of the revival under Josiah, kicked off by recovering "the Book of the Law of the LORD given through Moses" (2 Chr 34:14). In contrast, chapter 36 ends the Writings by saying three times (36:5, 9, 12) that the kings who followed Josiah "did evil in the sight of the LORD." The explanation for the exile is, "But they kept mocking the messengers of God, despising his words and scoffing at his prophets, until the wrath of the LORD rose against his people, until there was no remedy" (2 Chr 36:16). The Writings end asserting Torah neglect as the explanation for Israel's destruction.[31]

Further, the Torah promise that those who obey the *torah* will "prosper" (*tsalach*) while those who disobey "will not prosper" (Deut 28:19) is a major theme of Chronicles, with *tsalach* occurring 13 times![32] The word first appears about Solomon in 1 Chronicles 22:11: "you will prosper (*tsalach*) if you are careful to observe the statutes and the rules that the LORD commanded Moses for Israel. Be strong and courageous. Fear not; do not be dismayed" (1 Chr 22:13). The author reinforces the theme by repeating it over many chapters with many individuals. Quoting Joshua 1:9, "Be strong. . . . do not be dismayed," ties Tanak's end to the Prophets' beginning, binding them together as two units with the same message: obey the Torah and you will succeed![33] "It's like déjà vu all over again."

30. Alden, *Malachi,* 212.

31. "The king did evil in the sight of the Lord" is shorthand for departure from the Torah since half of the original Torah instructions for the coming kings (Deut 17:14–20) are about knowing and obeying the Torah.

32. See 1 Chronicles 22:11, 13; 29:23; 2 Chron 7:11; 13:12, 14:7; 18:11, 14; 20:20; 24:20; 26:5; 32:21; 32:30.

33. *Inclusio* is an ancient literary device that begins and ends a literary unit with the same words. It is also called "framing" or "bracketing." See Harvey, *Listening,* 102–3. Beyond signaling the limits of a literary unit, it often summarizes the content as Isaiah 1:2 and 66:24 communicate that Israel's history is characterized by that attitude.

THE LOGIC OF THE STRUCTURE OF THE HEBREW BIBLE

We can now state the logic of the Tanak structure.[34] The Torah introduces the main characters and themes, establishing where the story will go. The Prophets and the bulk of the Writings develop the Torah themes and the Latter Writings conclude the story. The Torah is *the* instruction in story form and Tanak is commentary and exposition of the story. The Prophets chronicle the fulfillment of the Torah's prediction that Israel will be scattered among the nations (Deut 28:15–68; 31:27–29) and explain "the mess Israel is in" as due to covenant failure (Deut 28:15–68). The Former Writings explain the Torah's wisdom for living in a sinful world.

Law	Former Prophets	Latter Prophets	Former Writings	Latter Writings
Genesis Exodus Leviticus Numbers Deuteronomy	Joshua Judges (1–2) Samuel (1–2) Kings	Isaiah Jeremiah Ezekiel The Twelve	Psalms Job Proverbs Ruth Song of Songs Ecclesiastes Lamentations Esther	Daniel Ezra-Nehemiah (1–2) Chronicles
"Instruction"	Narrative	Commentary	Exposition	Narrative
God's foundational instruction revealed	Torah's prediction of Israel's covenant failure documented in history	Torah's prediction of Israel's covenant failure explained as neglect of Torah	Explanation of how the godly are to live as they wait for God's promises to be fulfilled	Torah's themes of "the end of days," the restoration of God's people, and Torah neglect concluded

The Tanak story parallels the story in the Torah. Both begin by relating the origins of the universe and of Israel. The Torah ends with Israel preparing

34. Significantly adapted from DeRouchie, *Understand*, 25–26.

to enter Canaan after being excluded by God for her disbelief at Kadesh Barnea. Tanak ends with Israel preparing to enter the land again after being expelled during the exile (Chronicles). In other words, the Torah is the core revelation and Tanak shows that Israel's history reenacts the Torah story.[35] Both end looking forward in hope. This means, as Yogi Berra once said, that the future isn't what it used to be! In the future, approaching the Bible armed with this new perspective, you should read with new eyes and see new things. Reading the Bible in the Tanak order means your future isn't what it used to be.

35. Once again, I am indebted here to DeRouchie, *Understanding*, 23–26 and to Dempster, *Dominion and Dynasty*.

Chapter 5

The Message of Genesis: Finding Life

Genesis Brief Summary: Sin brings death; God promises to restore life.

When the first *Star Wars* film was released in 1977 it introduced the main themes and major characters that would dominate the trilogy it began (episodes IV, V and VI). We learn about the Force and midi-chlorians and we meet Luke and Leia and their friends. Beginnings do that! The first chapter of a novel or a television pilot sets the stage for the story in the same way.

The Torah is the beginning of the Hebrew Bible. As the beginning, it introduces the main themes that will be worked out through the Prophets and the Writings. Genesis is the beginning of the beginning! So, Genesis takes pride of place in the Torah because it announces many of the key themes that will animate the Hebrew and Christian Bibles. It establishes more of the principal themes than any other Torah unit. Further, it ushers onto the stage a number of the characters who will become permanent points of reference for Jews and Christians, such as Adam, Noah and Abraham. Genesis merits special attention as the beginning of the beginning.[1]

This chapter will determine the message of Genesis, i.e., its meaning for contemporary believers. To accomplish this, we will examine (1) the

1. "Genesis, the first book of the Bible, deals with themes and events that lay the foundation for the rest of Scripture. As the first words of the book suggest ("In the beginning"), Genesis introduces many theological threads that are woven throughout the tapestry of the entire Bible," Grisanti, *Word and World*, 170.

structure and (2) themes of the book. Then we will (3) state the message that arises from the structure and themes. We will end examining (4) how Christians see Jesus in the book. This will be our approach with each Torah unit. After we have studied all the Torah units, we will elaborate a comprehensive message for the Torah.

THE STRUCTURE OF GENESIS

Yogi Berra said that you can observe a lot by just watching! There are two things we should watch authors do because they are the tools that craft their message: *what* they say and *how* they say it, i.e., selection and arrangement.[2] What an author selects to include is important, but how he says it (structure) shapes and colors how we understand it.[3] To say "God knows the future, so he can be trusted to get us ready to face it" is a biblical truth. But to say the same thing differently can make a difference: "God is always preparing us for what he has prepared for us." We will investigate first *how* Genesis is structured and then *what* themes it develops.

The Structure of Genesis: The Arrangement of the Book

When examining the structure of a biblical book we must seek arrangements that were familiar to the original audience. Fortunately, we know a great deal about these.[4] Some structures the biblical authors used are familiar to us, like devoting space to what matters. But some are less familiar (e.g., artistic repetition), or completely unfamiliar (chiastic structures).[5] In an oral culture, where books were written to be *heard* when read out loud, such devices were aimed at the *ear*. Some of these translate (like repetition), while others do not (rhymes). So, those who read the biblical languages help us here. Detecting structure is an inductive process: we listen to the author rather than imposing our expectations upon him.

We have seen that "these are the generations of" structures Genesis. But the structure is more complex. Some of the *toledot* units start with the word "and," indicating that they "are intentionally linked to the *toledot* units

2. See Kaiser, *Exegetical Theology*, 205–8.

3. Dorsey, *Literary Structure*, 17.

4. There is an extensive literature, particularly for narrative literature, which is the genre (type of literature) of the Torah: see, e.g., Alter, *Art*; Bar-Efrat, *Narrative Art*.

5. In an oral culture biblical authors used many forms of repetition for emphasis. Chiastic structures are a form of repetition in which the elements in the first half of a unit are repeated in reverse order in the second half.

that precede."[6] Further, 5:1 and 11:10 are parallel[7] showing that 5:1 and 11:10 introduce parallel sections. The resulting outline of Genesis follows.

1. The creation story (1:1—2:3; not a *toledot* unit)
2. The *Toledot* of the heavens and the earth (2:3—4:26)
3. *Toledot* units 2 through 4 (5:1—11:9)
4. 5:5—6:8: *Toledot* of Adam (a linear genealogy, then the story of Noah)
5. 6:9—9:29: *Toledot* of Noah (the story of the flood)
6. *and* 10:1—11:9: *Toledot* of Ishmael (a segmented genealogy; the story of Babel)
7. *Toledot* units 5–10 (11:10—50:26)
8. 11:10: *Toledot* of Shem (a linear genealogy)
9. *and* 11:27: *Toledot* of Terah (the story of Abraham)
10. *and* 25:12: *Toledot* of Ishmael (a segmented genealogy)
11. *and* 25:19: *Toledot* of Isaac (the story of Isaac and [mostly] Jacob)
12. *and* 36:1–8, 36:9—37:1: *Toledot* of Esau (2 units: a story, then a genealogy)
13. 37:2: *Toledot* of Jacob (the story of Joseph)[8]

THE THEMES OF GENESIS

The Major Theme: Life vs. Death

The major theme of Genesis becomes clear from the big picture painted by the book.

6. DeRouchie, "The Blessing-Commission, 219–47; the quotation is on 232–33. I follow DeRouchie on Genesis's structure. The word "and" precedes *toledot* in 10:1; 11:27; 25:12; 25:19; and 36:1.

7. They are the only two linear genealogies in the *toledot* units. A linear genealogy moves rapidly by naming one person per generation. A segmented genealogy names numerous descendants in each generation. Also, both begin without the word "and." Both also trace the chosen line of blessing Finally, the last person in each genealogy has three sons.

8. DeRouchie, "Blessing Commission," 243, significantly adapted.

1. *The Creation Story (1:1—2:3)*

Genesis 1 is the beginning of the beginning of the beginning. It explains why God created the cosmos: he constructed a temple-house where he could dwell among his people.[9] Living among his people was the grand design. He carefully prepared it to be a good environment for human life (Gen 1:2–26) and service to God (Gen 1:26—2:3). Humans were created to represent God as his "image" by ruling the creation for him and spreading his kingdom (1:26–28). The original audience recognized Eden as a temple where God would dwell among his people.

2. *The Toledot of the Heavens and the Earth (2:4—4:26)*

The opening *toledot* unit stands alone. It discloses what became of the good world God had created. It elaborates on Gen 1 by saying that God created a lush environment for human enjoyment (2:4–14) and labor in God's service (2:15–24), requiring only obedience (2:16–17). But yielding to temptation, Adam and Eve preferred to believe what they preferred to be true. They doubted God and disobeyed, bringing alienation from God, other people, and the environment. Their sin also introduced dysfunction in all realms and ended in death (3:1–19). Since sin entered the world, life is like licking honey off a thorn: sweet, but punctuated by pain.

But God immediately promised to provide a remedy for this disaster (3:15), a promise met with faith by Adam (3:20), to which God responded with grace even in his judgment (3:21–24). But others responded to God's grace with further rebellion and violence, even while carrying out God's commands to fill and subdue the earth (4:1–26; 1:26–28).

3. *Toledot Units 2 through 4 (5:1 to 11:9), which Focus on Death*

Toledot units 2 through 4 hang together as a unit and emphasize judgment and death as results of sin. God announced that eating the forbidden fruit (his only prohibition!) would surely bring death (2:17),[10] but when eating "opened the eyes" with awareness of "nakedness" (3:7), one might conclude that God's threat was forgotten. Not so! The three units beginning at 5:1,

9. For temple imagery see Beale and Gladd, *Story Retold*, 1–4; Beale, *Temple*, 81–121. For "house" imagery see Leithart, *House*, 43–50; Morales, *Leviticus*, 39–41. Both images will be developed later.

10. "You shall surely die" (Gen 2:17) is a death sentence: "you are doomed to die," Alter, *Moses*, 21.

6:9, and 10:1 display a uniform trajectory: each begins with something good God created and ends with humans ruining it through sin. They emphasize death as the destiny of all people (5:1—6:8), twice displaying death by judgment (6:8—9:29; 10:1—11:9). Progressive deterioration is spotlighted when the first unit ends with a note of hope (6:8; as did 4:26) that is missing from the other two (9:29; 11:5–9). In fact, 10:1—11:9 concludes this unit of Genesis with a reversal of the creation account (an "uncreation").[11] The order-from-chaos theme of Genesis 1 is reversed. The penalty is not exactly, "Do not pass Go; do not collect $200." Human life continues and people pass Go and go on living, for a while. But death is the debt that all men pay, eventually.

4. Toledot Units 5 through 10 (11:10–50:26), which Focus on Life

The bulk of Genesis (*toledot* units 5 through 10) paints a starkly different portrait: God bringing life out of the death, thus reversing the trajectory of the last two sections (2:4—4:26; 5:1—11:9). Each major section starts at a low point produced by sin and proceeds upward to the blessing and life that God alone can bring. The Abraham story (*toledot* of Terah) begins with a barren wife and two funerals (11:27–32), pictures of death, and ends with a list of Abraham's many children (25:1–11), life out of death! The story of Isaac and Jacob also begins with a barren wife (25:21) and ends with a long list of children (35:23–26). The story of Joseph begins with his brothers threatening death (37:18–20) and ends with Joseph saving lives. The author uses Joseph's statement at the book's end to summarize the message of Genesis: "You planned evil against me; God planned it for good to bring about the present result—the survival of many people (Gen 50:20, HCSB). Genesis is about God bringing life from death. There are other themes, but most of the book is devoted to God bringing life out of death. This theme frames the book: Genesis begins with God creating life (Gen 1) and it ends with God restoring life out of death (Gen 50). The last *toledot* reverses the first. The first *toledot* unit (2:4—4:26) begins with Eden and spirals down to brother killing brother, while the last one (37:2—50:26) begins with brother plotting to kill brother but ends with God preserving life in Egypt![12] This theme is like Luke Skywalker in Star Wars Episodes IV–VI: *the* central focus.

11. Ross, *Creation*, 80.

12. Ross, *Creation*, 65–69. Ross points out that life-death, blessing-curse, and good-evil are three ways Genesis presents this duality. Life-death seems the book's main emphasis.

The Important Subthemes

As Han Solo is a less central character than Luke Skywalker, so, too, Genesis has less-central themes. These subthemes function in a supporting role. They are: God's presence; the reign, or kingdom of God (Gen 1); God's promise (Gen 3); faith and obedience (Gen 3); God's covenants (Gen 6, 9, 15, 17); and God's (and our) mission. We will peruse each one succinctly.

God's Presence

God's presence is surely *the* greatest treasure humans can know! He created all that exists (Gen 1:1) and his presence is announced in the first sentence of Genesis, so it must be a central theme! He is *the* source of all the good things humans can experience. He created beauty and all things functional in the garden he made for people to enjoy (Gen 2:9). Many people think of God as being as joyful as a Vulcan. No way! God created people like himself, so the human capacity for joy in intimate relationships and in meaningful labor (Gen 1, 2) could only mimic his nature. All the good things humans experience are a pale reflection of what God experiences, since his nature and experience are the source of all he created. He also created us for friendship with himself (Gen 3:8). The lush descriptions of Eden, with its trees, life-giving rivers and gold all reflect the blessings of God's presence.[13] God's presence is what made Eden a paradise.

The problem in Genesis 3:1–7 was that humans disobeyed God because they didn't trust him. God's sentence had a delivery like a brick through a plate-glass window: expulsion from the God's presence, and ultimate death (Gen 2:17; 3:19; 3:22–24) since God is the source of life! Being cut off from God is not like skipping church ("Wow, I can finally *enjoy* myself on Sunday!"). It is to be exiled to the wilderness, unplugged from the power source, condemned to live where "it is always winter and never Christmas."[14]

The Reign of God

The reign of God, or his kingdom, is universally acknowledged as a central biblical theme, and is seen by many as the "biblical center."[15] It is *logically more important* than the life-death theme, even though Genesis accentuates

13. Wenham, *Genesis*, 1:76.

14. Lewis, *The Lion, the Witch, and the Wardrobe*.

15. This author adopts this view. For a presentation of all Old Testament theology organized around this, see Merrill, *Everlasting Dominion*.

life vs. death. The theme begins in Genesis 1, where God is presented as king. After creating, God names what he creates, seen in the ANE as a function of the authority figure. Then Genesis 1:26 reads, "God said, "Let us make man . . . and let them have dominion." Who can grant authority to exercise dominion except the a king? The Torah ends with Deuteronomy, which is structured as a treaty between God as king and Israel as his subjects.[16] That means that the Torah begins and ends presenting God as king!

How is God's reign spread throughout the earth? This is why God created human beings. God explains the human mandate the instant he creates humans: "God said, 'Let us make man in our image, after our likeness. And let them have dominion. . . .' And God said to them, 'Be fruitful and multiply and fill the earth and subdue it and have dominion'" (Gen 1:26–28).

How do humans do this?[17] Hart argues that the "image of God" is not a description of human nature (such as, "humans have intellect, emotion and will").[18] Instead, as the ANE audience understood, it is a functional description: humans act as God's vice-regents, representing him like an ambassador, spreading his rule by "subduing and exercising dominion" over the earth (Gen 1:26, 28). "Dominion" is a kingly term and God commissions humans (males and females!) to "exercise dominion over" or "manage"[19] his creation. This "cultural mandate" is a *magna carta* for all cultural and scientific progress in order to utilize the latent potential God built into the environment. In the ANE an "image" (Gen 1:26) was a statue of a monarch erected to remind the populace who was their king. It was believed to be filled with his "spirit" or "breath" (same word in Hebrew, *ruach*).[20] Here Moses writes a polemic, an argument that draws from common knowledge but stands it on its head by presenting it with an unexpected twist. "Image" brings to the audience's mind a stone or metal statue of a king. He is declaring that humans are actually the statue of God on the earth, but a living statue, filled with his spirit (Gen 2:7).[21] Humans represent his rule by stepping off the pedestal and going to work extending his rule everywhere and in every field of endeavor ("subduing the earth"). Subduing means understanding it, mastering its use, and managing it. So, man is not "made *in*

16. See the chapter on Deuteronomy.

17. Dempster has written an excellent exposition of this in his *Dominion and Dynasty*.

18. Hart, "Genesis," 315–36. Merrill also argues this in *Everlasting Dominion* as does Ross in *Creation*.

19. Hart shows that "manage" is a good contemporary translation of the Hebrew term translated "have dominion": "Genesis," 323.

20. Hart, "Genesis," 317–24.

21. This was initially true of all humans; now it is true in the fullest sense only of believers.

the image of God" but "made *as* the image of God," that is, *to be his image.*[22] The Bible grants a far more exalted calling to humans than any other ANE religion. We are kings and queens of Narnia!

Dempster shows that there are two subthemes that advance God's kingdom. He calls them "dominion and dynasty."[23] We have just described "dynasty," i.e., the rule of humans over God's creation. Genesis says a great ruler will come through a dynasty descended from the tribe of Juda to reign over the world (Gen 49:10).[24] The term Genesis introduces for this dynasty leading to the promised one is "seed." That is why Genesis traces lineages so often. "Seed" is a major subtheme in Genesis, traced through time until it leads to the promised king.

Dempster's other subtheme is "dominion," by which he means the *place* where the dynasty will rule. The term for this in Genesis is "land." With Adam it was the Garden; with Israel it becomes the promised land; but the entire earth is ultimately the goal (Gen 49:10).

Promise

As soon as sin enters the picture, God makes a promise to eventually destroy the evil that began in the Garden, thus restoring his reign. Speaking to the serpent, God promised, "I will put enmity between you and the woman and between your offspring and her offspring; he shall bruise your head and you shall bruise his heel" (Gen 3:15). This first promise of a future deliverance has been recognized by Jews since at least the third century BC as the beginning of the messiah theme in Scripture.[25] This pregnant text casts a long shadow from Genesis forward, giving birth to further promises that expanded it (e.g., Isaiah 9:6–7). The dark side is doomed!

The promise theme is so prominent in Scripture that Kaiser, a major Old Testament scholar, sees it as the biblical center.[26] Kaiser is correct that God's one promise in Gen 3:15 becomes the fountainhead of the many promises and biblical covenants that later develop it. It is God's plan of

22. For a detailed explanation of this, and a perceptive theology of the entire Old Testament, see Merrill, *Everlasting Dominion*. This view of the image of God is now the dominant understanding among OT scholars.

23. Dempster, *Dominion and Dynasty*.

24. The structure of the passages shows that Gen 49:10 is the first exposition of Genesis 3:15, God's first promise.

25. Wenham, *Pentateuch*, 23: the *protoevangelium*, "first announcement of the gospel."

26. See Kaiser, *Promise-Plan*.

redemption[27] and is summarized by NT authors as "the promise" (e.g., Acts 26:6–7; Romans 4:13–14, 20; Hebrews 6:13–14). Other terms such as "blessing" are subthemes under the grand promise-theme.[28] Finally, Kaiser writes that "the culmination of all the specifications . . . are wrapped up in the one promise doctrine, or promise-plan, which focuses on Jesus Christ."[29] The end of the promise is that God will wipe away every tear (Revelation 21:4)!

Salvation

Implied in the life and promise themes, and reflected in the faith theme below, is the theme of salvation.[30] Merrill correctly asserts that the first example of this salvation "is the clothing of man and woman with animal skins graciously provided by the LORD" (Gen 3:21).[31] God will keep saving, but the prototype of God's salvation will come in Exodus.

Faith and Obedience

Faith is often thought of as belief without evidence in someone who speaks without knowledge of things without parallel. Even worse, "faith is believing what you know ain't so." This *is not* the Bible's view, as the first case of Bible faith shows. Part of God's promise to Eve was that she would live to bear children (3:16).[32] This promise elicited faith from Adam, as well as a corresponding action that showed his faith. "Adam named his wife Eve because

27. Kaiser, *Promise-Plan*, 19.

28. Kaiser, *Promise-Plan*, 20–25. Kaiser argues (35) that in Genesis "blessing" (used 88 times) is the promise term.

29. Kaiser, *Promise-Plan*, 25.

30. Merrill, *Biblical Theology*, 22, says correctly that salvation "is obviously a major theme of Biblical theology, though it clearly is not *the* central motif. This is evident in that salvation implies deliverance *from* something *to* something," meaning that it restores humans to a capacity they lost: to serve God.

31. Merrill, *Biblical Theology*, 22.

32. Sadly those children would now be sinners and bring pain along with their joy. This is the meaning of Gen 3:16. The Hebrew is a complex figurative sentence, literally, "I will increase your pain and your conception." "Pain and conception" are a hendiadys, a figure where two terms are used to describe on thing. It means "pain related to (what comes from) conception," i.e., children. Clarence Darrow's line arose from the truth in this passage: "The first half of our life is ruined by our parents and the second half by our children." But the curse is not the end.

[he believed that] she would become the mother of all the living" (Gen 3:20). This first faith text defines it: faith is counting God trustworthy.[33]

Notice that the author *shows* that Adam believed by telling us what he *did*. Naming his wife was an act motivated by trust in God's promise! Notice the order: faith produced obedience—an act that grew out of faith. This is the regular biblical pattern. Faith is the root and obedience is the fruit. Faith is the foundation and obedience the superstructure that rises from it. The most famous OT passage about faith (Gen 15:6) is a response to a promise of God. Faith in God's promise makes a person righteous, i.e., deemed to measure up to God's standard despite their sins. Abraham's faith yielded obedience (12:1–4). Henceforth, Abraham is the exemplar of faith (Romans 4:16). The Torah is punctuated by a series of faith texts that reiterate this vital theme: Exodus 4:5; 4:31; 14:31; Numbers 14:11; 20:12; Deuteronomy 1:32; 9:23.[34] Faith and obedience play a *major* role in the Bible, representing the foremost things God wants from us.

When he tempted Eve, the serpent was as subtle as a Smith & Wesson. *The* lie in the Garden was that disobedience to God is the route to real joy and the good life (Gen 3:4–6). It is still *the* lie that underlies all temptation (see John 8:44). Genesis is no less subtle: it shouts that obedience to God is what is good for us! A Torah core conviction is that obedience to God is beneficial for individuals and nations. Genesis is a long exercise in watching the results of obedience and disobedience work out in people's lives. Eve learned this: she saw what looked good (delicious fruit), but it turned out to be bad. Eve's problem was that she believed her senses and the voices of those around her rather than trusting God. Too bad she didn't know Obi-Wan Kenobi's advice: "Your eyes can deceive you. Don't trust them." Eve climbed what she believed to be the ladder of success only to find that it was leaning against the wrong wall. We, too, often get confused about "good." If someone shot their grandmother at 500 yards, they would be a good shot, but not a good person. Genesis defines "good" as trusting and obeying to God.

The biblical motivation for obedience is trust that God always works for our good (Romans 8:28).[35] In fact, there is a great deal of empirical evidence (evidence from careful social science research) that obedience to God's commands benefits people. For example, married people (marriage is God's idea) are healthier, happier, and live longer than single people.[36] This

33. The Hebrew term "faith" means to count as reliable.

34. Sailhamer, *Pentateuch*, 60 and note 101.

35. For a biblical argument that Paul's NT commands are meant to produce our flourishing, see Charry, *Renewing*.

36. See Waite and Gallagher, *Case for Marriage*; see further Stark, *America's Blessings*.

makes sense, since God knows everything and cares deeply for us. God also knows that if we love him, we will do for nothing what others will not do for anything.

Winston Churchill said that a fanatic is a man who can't change his mind but won't change the subject. By that definition Genesis is fanatical: it has the same mind as Joshua 1:8: obey the Torah and you will succeed. It won't change the subject either: faith is the root of which obedience is the fruit. But an idea can be relevant whether uttered BC by fourteen-century Israel or AD by Twenty-First-Century Fox. This idea is perpetually relevant because God said it.

Covenant

Abraham Lincoln said that commitment is what transforms a promise into a reality. A promise of love is transformed into the reality of marriage by a commitment ceremony called a wedding. God committed himself to humans so that his promises would become reality. His commitments are called "covenants." A covenant is an agreement to obligate oneself to someone or something. The OT uses the term for friendship agreements (1 Samuel 18:3), treaties (Gen 21:27) and for marriage contracts (Malachi 2:14).[37] But its most important use is in describing a series of covenants God makes with humans. God's covenant first appears in Gen 6, then in Gen 9, 15, 17. Its centrality is universally acknowledged. McConville observes that "Covenant as a theological idea is distinctly biblical."[38] Other ANE religions did not conceive of their gods making agreements with people, so this OT uniqueness highlights the importance of "covenant." Covenants are the engine that runs the train, animating the biblical plot from start to finish.[39]

One striking feature of Genesis is that it narrates *several* covenants! T. David Gordon has argued that there are three primary covenants in the Bible. He calls these Promise, Law, and Faith. Broadly, Promise is God's covenant with Abraham to give him descendants (seed) in a land where they would be a blessing to the entire world (Genesis 12:1–3). Law is his covenant with Moses that is summarized in the Ten Words given at Mount Sinai. Faith is Jeremiah's New Covenant that replaces the Mosaic covenant (Jeremiah 31:31–33), inaugurated by Jesus (Luke 22:20; 1 Corinthians

37. McConville, "Covenant/*berit*," 1:748.

38. McConville, "Covenant/*berit*," 1:753.

39. See Merrill, *Everlasting Dominion*, 293.

11:25).[40] God's middle name is not, "Obey, obey, obey, I say!" His covenants commit him to our wellbeing as we trust and obey him.

Mission

Throughout Genesis there is also an emphasis on the nations as the intended recipient of Israel's mission. God's intent was always that Israel bear witness to the grandeur of her God in order to draw the nations to him. One of the ways this is evident is the structure of Genesis: By framing the focus on Israel with sections on the nations and by ending Genesis with serving God by serving a pagan nation, the book keeps the nations before the audience.[41] DeRouchie makes a good case that the genealogies dealing with those outside the line of blessing (10:1; 25:12; 36:1) are there to remind Israel of her obligation to be evangelists.[42]

Genesis 1–11	Genesis 12–36	Genesis 37–50
The nations	Israel	The nations

THE MESSAGE OF GENESIS

The message of Genesis: God created the world as a temple-house where he could live in intimate friendship with the people he created. They would serve him in his temple as human agents of his reign, worshipping him, extending his kingdom, and finding abundant life in him. But sin entered God's house and brought death: alienation from God, from other people, and from God's good gifts. God responded by making a promise to defeat evil, to which he called people to respond with faith and obedience so that they could be renewed in life, and he made covenants with those who believed,[43] *promising friendship with him and blessing. He also called believers to a mission to share their great God and his promise with the nations.*

Genesis one-sentence summary: God created the world to live with his people and bless them; when sin brought death into his house, God began fulfilling a promise to restore life that comes by trusting God and obeying his commands.

40. Gordon, *Promise.*

41. I owe this observation to Hamilton, *Genesis,* 10, by way of DeRouchie, "Blessing-Commission," 240–41.

42. DeRouchie, "Blessing-Commission," 238–42.

43. Some covenants, like the one with Noah, are not dependent upon faith.

Genesis Brief Summary: Sin brings death; God promises to restore life.

WHERE WE SEE JESUS IN GENESIS

Christians see Jesus everywhere in Genesis! This should be so if the thesis of this book is correct—that the Torah is the heart of the Hebrew Bible and that the entire OT is about Jesus as he himself said (Luke 24:25–27, 44–45). Here are some ways Christians see Jesus in Genesis.

Life-Death/Blessing-Curse

Life and death and how we obtain them is *the* key theme of Genesis. God wants us to experience life, real life, his kind of life, the sort of life Adam experienced before he sinned. God is the source of all life, so it is no surprise that Jesus would say, "I came that they may have life and have it abundantly" (John 10:10). In fact, "life" is the central theme of the Gospel of John, where Jesus also said, "This is eternal life, that they know you, the only true God and Jesus Christ whom you have sent" (John 17:3). Jesus is the source of life! In John "eternal life" is literally "the life of the age (to come)" (Greek *zoe aion*). The Jews divided history into two ages: the present age and the age to come (the age of messiah). By "eternal life" John means not simply "life that lasts for eternity," but the life of God that makes one fit to enter the messianic age, or we might say, heaven. Jesus restores God's life to all who believe (John 1:12).

Reign of God and the Messiah-King

God is the High King over the sea and Jesus is Aslan.[44] A king's job is to exercise authority to bring harmony, peace and human well-being (Hebrew *shalom*). Jesus is the one promised in Genesis 3:15, who will someday put the world to rights and destroy the dark side. Jesus is the Lion of the tribe of Judah (Gen 49:8–12; Revelation 5:5), the Prince of Peace (Isaiah 9:6–7) who will make wars cease (Isaiah 2:2–4). Matthew expounds upon Jesus' kingship. Scripture's king theme and all the shortcomings of human authorities through history are invitations to yearn for the one who will bring permanent justice and peace (Isaiah 9:6–7).[45]

44. See Lewis, *The Chronicles of Narnia*.

45. Excellent treatments of the messiah theme in the OT are Kaiser, *Rediscovering*, 101–20 and Kaiser, *Messiah*.

Faith and Obedience

God requires obedience, which we cannot achieve (Romans 7:14–25). Jesus fully trusted God and so was fully obedient to God (Hebrews 4:15). His obedience is credited to the believer's account so that we have a righteousness that exceeds that of the scribes and Pharisees (Matt 5:20). James 2:14–26 gleans its message from Genesis: faith is the root, obedience its fruit.

Mission

The mission of Israel to share the good news about their God was accomplished by Jesus. Yet he calls Christians to join with him in that same mission until he returns to establish his kingdom in its fullness (Isaiah 52:7; Luke 4:19; Matthew 28:19–20).

OTHER GLIMPSES OF JESUS OR NEW TESTAMENT

Biblical Typology

An important way Christians see Jesus in Genesis is in typology, a strategy used by the biblical authors whereby they point out parallels between earlier and later things. Wenham points out that the Abraham, Jacob, and Joseph stories in Genesis have many parallels with each other, such as each story beginning with a divine revelation and each major character being called to leave his home.[46] Beale defines typology as involving (a) analogies between people, events and institutions and (b) foreshadowing of future things in past things.[47] This happens within Genesis and across Scripture as well, for example, when later biblical authors like Isaiah see Israel's distant future as a (better) reenactment of the Exodus from Egypt. This strategy is widespread in Scripture, explaining how the NT authors detected foreshadowing of Jesus in OT institutions (like the Davidic kingship), or OT events (like Jesus' forty days in the wilderness as parallel to Israel's forty years in the wilderness: Mark 1:1–13). Wenham observes, "There are also parallels between the lives of these patriarchs and the subsequent history of Israel: in other words, the patriarchs are not simply individuals in their own right but embodiments of the nation."[48] The same is true of Jesus: he is the embodiment

46. See Wenham, *Pentateuch*, 36; Wenham, *Genesis 1–11*, 256–58.

47. Beale, *Handbook*, 13–14. See also Beale and Gladd, *Story Retold*, 18–30.

48. Wenham, *Pentateuch*, 36.

of true humanity (Paul sees him as a second Adam) and of the ideal Israelite (Matthew sees Jesus' flight from Egypt as analogous to Israel's exodus, Matthew 2:15, quoting Hosea 11:1).[49] Examples in Genesis include Jesus as a priest after the order of Melchizedek (Hebrews 5:6) and Jesus as the ideal human ("image of God," Gen 1:26; Colossians 1:15).

Adam

Paul cites Jesus as a second Adam, the one who accomplished what Adam failed to do (1 Cor 15:45). Adam failed to spread God's kingdom everywhere, but that mandate continued for all sons of Adam and daughters of Eve (Psalm 8). Paul tells us that Jesus will fulfill the human destiny of ruling when he establishes his kingdom in its fullness and God's reign by humans is inaugurated (Ephesians 1:19–23, quoting from Psalm 8:6; Revelation 20:1–6).

Eden

Eden means "delight." Eden was a perfect environment and sin's effects mean that we live east of Eden and hunger to return to paradise. Jesus' work will restore Eden, as the edenic imagery throughout the second half of Revelation makes clear (e.g., Rev 22:4, 14, 19).

Image of God

Humans were created "as the image of God" (Gen 1:26). When we failed in that role, God determined that Jesus, *the* man, would do what humans failed to do and be (Colossians 1:15). He is the perfect manifestation of God (John 14:9).

Rest

God rested at the end of the creation story because there was no more bad to turn into good (Gen 1:31; 2:1–3). God's rest was a model for humans to rest regularly and the Torah was the first document in human history to mandate a weekly day of rest for humans! A day of rest is a gift of the

49. A treatment of this phenomenon covering every OT use in the NT is found in Beale and Carson, *Commentary*.

Hebrew Bible to the world. Yet physical rest is only a symbol of a deeper, spiritual rest that comes from faith in Christ (Heb 4:9). Jesus, echoing God's achievement in Genesis 2, promised to grant that sort of rest to anyone who would come to him in faith (Matt 11:28).[50]

God's Self-Revelation

God's self-revelation first occurs in Genesis, then through prophets and in other ways. The Torah is the foundational written revelation of God. But the apex of God's revelation of himself was when Jesus came to earth, lived in a human body, walked and talked among us (Heb 1:1–3).[51] All biblical revelation points to Jesus because in the face of Jesus, we see God!

The Gospel

The Torah is good news ("gospel") about God's promise to rescue us from ourselves, our penchant for avoiding God (Gen 3:8), and our stubborn faith that disobedience to God will bring life to the full (Gen 3:4–6). That good news was always a word about Jesus Christ. Paul declared it: "Scripture, foreseeing that God would justify the Gentiles by faith, preached the gospel beforehand to Abraham, saying, 'In you shall all the nations be blessed'" (Galatians 3:8). Genesis is the first biblical testament to Jesus and what he offers to all who will believe!

MEDITATING ON TORAH DAY AND NIGHT

As a help toward meditating on Torah day and night, here is the key text of Genesis: Genesis 50:20.

50. "Land" and "rest" "emerge as the two dominant theological themes of the pre-monarchical era," i.e., Joshua, Judges and Samuel: Kaiser, *Theology*, 123. See Beale and Gladd, *Story Retold*, 374–5 for an exposition of "rest."

51. See Bird, *Evangelical Theology*, 164–213.

Chapter 6

The Message of Exodus: Courtship and Marriage

Exodus Brief Summary: God invites people into a committed relationship.

In *Star Wars* Episode II, Attack of the Clones, a child named Anakin Skywalker meets Queen Padme Amidala. After helping her escape danger, they are separated for a decade and Anakin joins the Jedi order, which disallows love and marriage for its members. But Anakin cannot stop thinking about her and his feelings for her grow. They meet again when the Jedi Council assigns him to protect now-senator Amidala from an assassination attempt and they go into hiding together. Time together draws each toward the other romantically, despite the Jedi prohibition and her belief that the relationship is ill-advised. Caught by the Republic and sentenced to death, Padme finally declares her love for Anakin. After their escape, encouraged by her admission, he woos her and works to persuade her that their relationship can work. He finally convinces her, and they marry, keeping it a secret lest he be expelled from the Jedi order.

Most people look forward to love and marriage like the pot of gold at the end of the rainbow. But getting there involves a process. It means getting to know one another and appreciating the benefits of a relationship with each other. These lead people to make a commitment. Like in Anakin and Padme's relationship, there are always complications. But when the benefits seem to outweigh the dangers, people commit themselves and begin living life together. This process is the story of Exodus. Alexander is on target when he declares, "Exodus is essentially a book about knowing God through personal experience."[1] But it is even deeper than that: it is the story of a marriage[2] between God and his people.

We must briefly justify the claim that Exodus is like a marriage between God and his people. Some may find this idea strange or even offensive, like a politician coming to a press conference in his underwear. Yet marriage imagery is widespread in the Bible. The Old Testament speaks in several places about God as a "husband" and Israel as his "wife" (e.g., Hosea 2:2, 7, 16; Ezekiel 16:1–43). The same image occurs in the New Testament, except that Jesus is the "bridegroom" and the church is his "bride" (Ephesians 5:21–33, esp. v. 32; Rev 19:7). Further, idolatry is often portrayed as spiritual "prostitution" (e.g., Ezekiel 16:30–31), or adultery (Ezek 16:33). Sometimes God's relationship with Israel looks like it is heading for a "divorce" (Isaiah 50:1; Jeremiah 3:8). So, the marriage image is justified.[3]

Where did biblical writers get the idea that God is like a husband to Israel? The answer is from Exodus! Hosea speaks of Israel's persistent spiritual adultery but then declares that God will woo Israel back to himself "as at the time when she came out of the land of Egypt" (Hos 2:15), that is, "after they were newly "married" in the covenant at Sinai."[4]

YOUR MISSION

Cole signaled the importance of Exodus when he called it "the center of the Old Testament." He added because the exodus event is "the supreme fact of all history," and is profoundly relevant to Christ, "no book, therefore, will more repay careful study, if we wish to understand the central message of the New Testament."[5]

1. Alexander, *Paradise*, 187.

2. This observation I owe to Leithart, *House*, 78, though I apply it more broadly than he does. Morales says: "the Mosaic covenant is likened to a marriage relationship elsewhere in Scripture. . . . then, on the threshold of consummation, Israel commits adultery on the nuptial night" when they build the golden calf: see Morales, *Leviticus*, 90.

3. Note that marriage is not the only biblical analogy for God's relationship with his people. For example, the image of Father and child is more common. Nevertheless, the husband-wife image is biblical and instructive.

4. See Stuart, *Hosea-Jonah*, 1988, 155, Kindle, commenting on Hosea 2:14. Jeremiah 31:32 speaks similarly.

5. Cole, *Exodus*, 18, 19, 18.

But more pointedly, "Mawwiage, mawwiage; mawwiage is what bwings us heow today."[6] So, in this chapter your mission, should you choose to accept it, is to track "Twue wove" in God's love relationship with his people and discover how God's love works even when his spouse isn't always faithful. A love relationship is stronger than an employer and employee relationship. God loves us and wants us to love him because he knows that if we love him, we will do for nothing what others will not do for anything. As with Genesis, we want to determine the message of Exodus for contemporary believers. Again, we will examine (1) the structure and (2) themes of the book. Then we will (3) state the message and end examining (4) how Christians see Jesus in Exodus.

THE STRUCTURE OF EXODUS

Exodus continues the Genesis story but introduces a new main character: Moses. Moses dominates the Torah like the President does a White House briefing. Wenham classifies the book as "Torah in the form of a biography of Moses."[7] Yet this is not quite accurate. The Torah is a quarter over before he appears.[8] Besides, Genesis is also largely a biography of Abraham and three generations of his descendants. So, a more accurate view is that the Torah is *instruction in the form of biographies, especially of Abraham and Moses.*

So, how is the biography of Moses in Exodus structured? Wenham says, "Unlike the book of Genesis Exodus has no titles for each new section. . . . Content, not form, must guide the definition of its parts."[9] Wenham also points out an important consideration about the content: "Exodus builds to its first climax at the Red Sea, but its second and even more important peak is the law-giving at Sinai."[10] That is, Exodus 1–15 is a unit concluded by Israel's reactions (Exod 15–18) and Exodus 19–24 is a unit. So, the content suggests the following structure:

1. God saves Israel from slavery: Exodus 1–18
2. God establishes a covenant to give his people good laws: Exodus 19–24

6. This is a line from the film, "The Princess Bride" (1987) written by William Goldman and directed by Rob Reiner. See https://www.imdb.com/title/tt0093779/, accessed Feb. 14, 2020.

7. Wenham, *Pentateuch*, 57.

8. Wenham, *Pentateuch*, 6. Genesis is 24 percent of the Torah.

9. Wenham, *Pentateuch*, 58.

10. Wenham, *Pentateuch*, 67.

3. Israel builds God a house so he can live with them: Exodus 25–40[11]

This accentuates three themes from Genesis that take center stage here: salvation, covenant, and the presence of God. Utilizing the marriage imagery, the book may be conceived this way: getting to know God deeply and personally, as in marriage,

1. Begins with getting to know each other (Exod 1–18);
2. Is sealed with a voluntary commitment ceremony (Exod 19–24); and
3. Involves preparing to live together in close relationship (Exod 25–40).[12]

MAJOR THEMES OF EXODUS

Exodus 1–18: Salvation: Getting to Know You

The road toward marriage begins with people getting to know each other. A relationship with God does also. Exodus 1–15 details Israel getting to know God, while Exodus 15–18 focuses on God getting to know Israel.

Exodus 1–15: Getting to Know God

Exodus 1–15 helps Israel to get to know God by chronicling the exodus from Egypt.[13] Israel had multiplied like rabbits over the course of 400 years living in the land of Egypt! They had grown up exposed to many gods ("polytheism") and many likely thought in those terms. If Israel is to embrace a relationship with God, she must learn how he is different from the

11. Wenham, *Pentateuch*, 58, adapted; see also Dillard and Longman, 62; Leithart, *House*, 71–86; and many scholars. Others outline it by the geographical locations in the book, e.g., Merrill et al., *Word and World*, 192. There is in fact substantial debate about the best way to outline Exodus. While we prefer this three-part structure, we will seek the themes that arise from the text without making our analysis dependent upon any one structure.

12. Stuart, *Exodus*, argues that Exod 6:6–8 is the key theological summary of Exodus: 34–40.

13. "Liberation theology," popular in the 1960s through the 1990s in some Latin American Roman Catholic circles, read Exodus as endorsing violence to liberate oppressed people from dictatorship. Although the problem was real, this solution is problematic on several counts, esp. that Exodus is not about political solutions for all people but addresses God's rescue of his chosen people (see Stuart, *Exodus*, 35, for rebuttal. Morales, *Leviticus*, 77, is right: "the major theme of the first half of Exodus is not liberation, but rather knowledge of YHWH."

gods of Egypt, as a woman who had a rotten boyfriend must learn to trust her new one. In fact, Pharaoh articulates the theme of this section: "Who is the LORD, that I should obey his voice and let Israel go?" (Exod 5:2).[14] Exodus 1–15 is the answer to Pharaoh's question. As the story proceeds, Israel becomes acquainted with her God. Note the recurrent phrase, "that you may know that I am the LORD" (e.g., Exod 6:7–8; 8:10, 22; 9:14, 29, etc.).[15] Israel comes to understand her past with God (Exod 3:6, 15) and that he remembers his promises (e.g., 2:24). In the plagues on Egypt, she sees that her God controls everything the "gods" of Egypt were supposed to control (Exod 12:12) and that he is the one, true God.[16] She witnesses his staggering power over nature (Exod 14). She sees that he is personal and loves her (Exod 4:22; 15:13; 34:7). Pharaoh and Egypt also see who God is (Exod 8:8; 9:16) and many Egyptians come to believe in the Lord (Exod 12:38). In fact, from the burning bush (Exod 2:3) to the explanation of God's name (Exod 3:14), to the Ten Words, the entire book constitutes an exposition of God's character.[17] But while *explaining* who God is has value, Exodus's primary strategy is to *show* who God is by portraying his interactions with people, both Pharaoh and God's "son" Israel. This strategy makes God's character clear in real-life situations. The portrait it paints is beautiful, deep and rich. The laws God gives (Exod 19–24) show Israel God's ideas and the tabernacle (Exod 25–40) unveils the experience of approaching God and living in his presence. So, the entire book answers Pharaoh's question, "Who is the LORD?" (Exod 5:2). The New Testament can be short because Exodus so vividly *showed* God's character. The believer who yearns to *really know* God in an ever-deepening love relationship should read Exodus. It is like listening to beautiful music and realizing when you listen again and again that there is far more beauty in it than you first perceived. Familiarity breeds deeper appreciation.

14. Fretheim, *Exodus*, 14.

15. Klein says this recurring phrase summarizes "the theological goal of the entire book." Cited by Morales, *Leviticus*, 79, note 8.

16. The "hardening" (better "strengthening") of Pharaoh's heart is a famous challenge in Exodus. Alexander (*Paradise*, 193–4) well says that this "is generally misunderstood, with many readers assuming that God caused Pharaoh to act against his own will. It is often suggested that although Pharaoh wanted to release the Israelites, God prevented him from doing this. However, a careful reading of the text reveals that by strengthening Pharaoh's heart, God actually enables him to remain true to his inner convictions. To this end, it is important to observe that the strengthening of Pharaoh's heart always comes after a hardship is removed and Pharaoh is no longer being pressured to release the Israelites. The motif of Pharaoh's heart being strengthened reveals that God wants the Egyptian king to release the Israelites willingly and not while under duress."

17. Cole, *Exodus*, 20–22.

Salvation

A major thing that Israel learns about God in Exodus 1–15 is that he saves. God is like a lifeguard: saving is his business. Salvation is a major theme of Exodus 1–15, since *knowing* God *is* salvation (e.g., John 17:3). Salvation in Exodus entails a nation being delivered from slavery. Yet it represents salvation of a deeper sort, of individuals being saved from slavery to their sins (e.g., Gen 15:6; Deut 6:25). Faith is foundational to both.[18]

The salvation theme is introduced as soon as sin alienates humans from God (Gen 3:15)[19] and grows from there,[20] but the grand biblical example of God's salvation is the exodus event in Exodus 1–15. "The exodus was God's greatest act of salvation in the Old Testament."[21] The fact that it occupies half of Exodus is a testimony to its centrality, as the size of Central Park testifies to the value placed upon it by New York City. So is the fact that it is told twice, once in prose (Exod 1–14) then again in poetry (Exod 15).[22] Both call it an act of salvation (Exod 14:13; 15:2), two of the earliest biblical uses of that term. It also provides the occasion for the first exposition of redemption (Exod 6:6; 13:13, 15; 21:30; 34:30). "The significance of the event is clearly seen in the way that the Exodus theme is constantly reapplied throughout the Old Testament and into the New. Indeed, this great act of salvation becomes the paradigm for future deliverances."[23] Israel's deliverance from Egypt is also replete with creation themes.[24] For example, the plagues are an uncreation, turning Egypt toward the original chaotic state of creation before God brought order while picturing what turning from God produces.[25]

18. Merrill, *Deuteronomy*, 176, explains that obedience demonstrates faith: "Thus the central feature of the covenant stipulations is their providing a vehicle by which genuine saving faith might be displayed (see Deut 24:13; Hab 2:4; Rom 1:17; 4:1–5; Gal 3:6–7).

19. For an excellent discussion of Gen 3:15 see Merrill, *Everlasting Dominion*, 246–48.

20. See Merrill, *Everlasting Dominion*, 228–37.

21. Dillard and Longman, *Introduction*, 65–66.

22. See Merrill, *Everlasting Dominion*, 264. Poetry in Scripture calls special attention to its subject.

23. Dillard and Longman, *Introduction*, 65–66. See also regarding the Passover: Alexander, *Paradise*, 206. For a study of how the Exodus echoes through the rest of Scripture see Estelle, *Echoes*.

24. Fretheim argues this at length in *Exodus*, 12–14.

25. Fretheim, "Exodus," 256.

PASSOVER

The exodus story is interrupted (Exod 12–13) by the first description of Passover.[26] At first that may seem like pausing to read a page from the phone book during a Mozart concert. But this must be important because the detailed Passover story is granted more space than the last plague and the exodus itself! In the story God destroys the first-born of Egypt, the climactic plague that echoes what Pharaoh had done to "God's son" (Exod 1:22; 4:23).[27] But God promises deliverance if his people will paint the blood of a sacrificed lamb on their door frames. God said (Exod 12:13), "The blood shall be a sign for you, on the houses where you are. And when I see the blood, I will pass over you and no plague will befall you to destroy you, when I strike the land of Egypt." This mighty act of God is the great biblical portrayal of substitutionary atonement, the guilty spared when an innocent (lamb) pays the just price (atone) by dying in their place. This echoes the "sacrifice" of Isaac, where a ram was substituted instead of Abraham's son (Gen 22).

This grand illustration of atonement is used in the New Testament to explain Christian salvation: Jesus is our Passover (Exod 12:21; 1 Cor 5:7; John 1:29).[28] Christian celebrations of Jesus' atoning death at the Lord's Table echo the Passover feast.[29]

FAITH IN EXODUS

Exodus continues Genesis's theme: obedience is the fruit, but faith is the root.[30]

Exodus 4:5	that [Israel] may believe that the LORD . . . has appeared to you [Moses]
Exodus 4:31	the people believed . . . and worshipped
Exodus 14:31	so, the people feared the LORD and they believed in the LORD and in Moses
Exodus 19:9	I am coming to you . . . that the people may hear and . . . believe you forever

26. Alexander, *Paradise*, chapter 14, is a fine treatment of the Passover.

27. Though God's mercy is shown in that Pharaoh killed all the male children whereas God kills only the first-born.

28. As Alexander points out, the ESV, NIV, etc., mistranslate 1 Cor 5:17 by adding "lamb"; the Greek says "Passover": *Paradise*, 202. Note 1.

29. For a comparison of Passover to Jesus' last supper and the Christian Lord's Supper see Alexander, *Paradise*, 206.

30. Sailhamer, *Meaning*, 344–48.

Exodus 15–18: Getting to Know Israel

In Exodus 15:22–18:27 God gets to know Israel. The bulk of the material is about Israel's poor character. The opening passage (15:22–27) bluntly contrasts the beautiful poetic expression of God's salvation (15:1–21) with Israel's grumbling against the Lord when the first test came. Chapters 16–17 repeat the exercise! God sees that *even after witnessing* his power in staggering miracles that defeated the most powerful ruler and army in the world, Israel is weak in faith and poor in obedience! They are as slow as a sloth to learn from what they have experienced! These incidents create Israel's reputation as a stubborn or "stiff-necked people" (Exod 32:9, etc.), a repeated Torah theme. Their doubt is subtle as an avalanche.

A great experience of God or act of faith is often followed by doubt or disobedience[31]								
Gen 12	Gen 20	Exod 15	Exod 16	Exod 17	Exod 32	Lev 10	Num 13–14	Num 21

Exodus starts with Israel building cities for Pharaoh and ends with her building a house for her God. Israel learns that God is a better master than Pharaoh. But God sees that Israel is as predictable as the weather. These truths will characterize God and Israel from here forward. God will be a good husband, but Israel will often be an unfaithful wife.

Exodus 19–24: Covenant: The Marriage of the Lord and Israel

Once two people know each other, a relationship which progresses to marriage is sealed with a voluntary commitment ceremony, a wedding. Now that Israel knows God's character, he invites them to confirm the covenant made with their ancestors. God issues his invitation after he sees their disbelief and grumbling: he knows their weaknesses (Psalm 103:14). They are invited in Exodus 19–24 to commit themselves to a permanent relationship with him based upon clear knowledge of his expectations. God proposes and they will accept.

Exodus 19–24 has three units: the Ten Words (Exod 19–20), the Book of the Covenant expanding them (20:22—23:33), and a covenant ratification ceremony (24).

31. Wenham, Pe*ntateuch*, 66.

Exodus 19–24: The Wedding

Leithart calls Exodus 20–24 "The Marriage Supper of Yahweh."[32] Marriage is seen in the Old Testament as a covenant (Malachi 2:14) and Leithart shows that the covenant in Exodus 19–24 (Exod 24:7) is written to sound like a wedding. That is why later biblical writers use "husband" and "wife" imagery (Ezekiel 16:1–14; Hosea 1–3). Moses is the officiating minister and he brings Israel the proposal: "Moses came and told the people all the words of the LORD and all the rules" (Exod 24:3). Then, Leithart observes, Israel essentially says, "I do." Leithart concludes, "The wedding ceremony ends with a wedding reception, a feast in the LORD's presence (Exodus 24:9–11)."[33] As in a marriage, God loves his people and wants them to love him. He knows that with love, his people will do for nothing what others will not do for anything. This picture is repeated in the New Testament with Jesus and his church (2 Cor 11:2; Ephesians 5:32) and Scripture ends with the Wedding Supper of the Lamb (Revelation 19:7–9).

Exodus 19–20: The Mosaic Law Covenant

With the Ten Words Exodus continues the Genesis theme of God's covenant. This section introduces and expounds upon the Mosaic Covenant, the dominant covenant after the Abrahamic Covenant. This is the focus of Exodus 19–24, and the Mosaic Covenant dominates the rest of the Old Testament. Having liberated Israel from Egypt, God gives to them good laws by which they can construct a social order that will bring blessing to the individual and the nation. Modern people often dislike rules, preferring maxims like, "Conscience is your compass." Such beliefs are blind to the influence of factors like tradition, history and religion upon what our conscience tells us. Moses' laws describe what faithfulness to God looks like.

It surprises some that the Ten Words are numbered differently by Jews and Christians.[34] Christians changed the Jewish numbering, likely because early English versions mistranslated "ten words" as "ten commandments," making the first "word" not seem like a "commandment." It says, "I . . . brought you out of the land of Egypt" (Exod 20:2). That difference

32. Leithart, *House*, 78–81. Alexander compares it to "making marriage vows" (*Paradise*, 188).

33. Leithart, *House*, 79.

34. In fact, Christians have *two* orders for the Ten Commandments because they divide them in different places. For a convenient summary chart see http://www.biblestudymagazine.com/extras-1/2014/10/31/counting-the-ten-commandments by Michael S. Helser (accessed 2–16–2020).

makes a difference! The Christian numbering begins with "You shall have no other gods," cementing the impression that the Ten Words are "laws," "commands." It makes them sound coercive and legalistic. But the Jewish numbering communicates differently. It makes plain that *it is because* God took the initiative and rescued Israel from slavery that he now invites them to accept his proposal and become his bride. God's goodness is the reason Israel should choose to follow God. That is a horse of a very different color!

If a male stranger came up to a woman he did not know and began giving her orders, she would be justified in saying, "You have no claim on me! I don't even know you!" But if that same man had wooed her, showed he loved her, been good to her, and had won her heart and then said, "Because you have seen that I love you, I ask you to marry me and choose to 'keep yourself only unto me as long as we both shall live,'" she would likely say "Yes!" What comes before the obligations makes all the difference! Marriage does entail many obligations, but when love is the motivator, we voluntarily, even cheerfully, take on obligations because *we want to*.

God invited Israel to become his bride because he loved her. But he also had a history with her and he had ridden in on his white steed and rescued the damsel in distress. He had whisked her away from her painful past and promised to take her to his castle in a beautiful land (Exod 3:8). He gave her new clothes and jewels (Exod 3:22). Then he said, "Here is what it means to be wed to me (Exod 20–24); will you accept?" The Ten Words are not harsh obligations imposed upon unwilling people; they are appropriate rules for a committed love relationship.

Note also that the Ten Words are listed in descending order of importance in two ways. One is that the Words regarding God come before those about obligations to humans, since putting God first is the best motivation for treating people well. Second, within each category (toward God and toward humans), the most important comes first and the least important is last. So, "have no other gods before me" (Exod 20:3) is logically prior to "You shall not take the name of the LORD your God in vain" (20:7). "Do not murder" (20:13) is more important than "Do not commit adultery" (20:14) and so on throughout both lists. Once this is seen, two fascinating things become apparent. First, the first Word is "I am the LORD your God, who brought you out of the land of Egypt, out of the house of slavery" (20:2). This shows again that acknowledging God's grace takes priority over simply obeying the rules that follow, as we have already seen.[35] Gratitude and love are the motivations God urges upon us. The other is that the first Word

35. Note Exodus 20:6, "showing steadfast love to thousands of those who *love* me and keep my commandments."

regarding humans is "Honor your father and our mother" (20:12). That this Word precedes "Do not murder" and all the others shows its priority over those Words! That's because honoring one's father and mother is the foundation for treating all people well. Those who honor this Word are less likely to disregard the other Words.[36]

Obedience to God is Beneficial

We have argued that the Ten Words and the Book of the Covenant (Deut 21–23) are like marriage vows: good rules adopted voluntarily to foster a strong love relationship. Exodus is *the* Bible portrait of how attachment to God is beneficial to us. (e.g., Deut 4:40).[37] Israel begins Exodus as slaves in Egypt.[38] But God's rescue of the nation and his tender care through their wilderness wanderings prove the benefits of attachment to him. Exodus is the story of God bringing slaves to freedom, the destitute to abundance, the vulnerable to security—life out of death. Thoreau once said that goodness is the only investment that never fails. The Exodus stories about obedience and disobedience to God are a biblical catechism in good investment, and in abundant life![39]

God's Words are also good for us in another sense: the essence of the Ten Words and the Book of the Covenant is instruction in how to love God and love one's neighbor.[40] These rules work for good personal relations and a happy social order.[41] The fact that the Ten Words are stated in the negative tends to obscure this from us. But four things should be noted. One is that a command stated in the negative is more concise.[42] Kaiser also observes that "moral law is always double sided. Every moral action is at the same time

36. Empirical research shows that people who attend church regularly are measurably less likely to be arrested, people who attend sporadically are more likely, and those who never attend are most likely.

37. Note the contrast: the Torah begins with Abraham seeking "that it may go well with me" by lying (Gen 12:13), and ends with God declaring "that it may go well with you" if we "keep his statutes and his commandments" (Deut 4:40).

38. These terrible realities have been all too common in the experiences of the Jews through history, in the African American community through American history, in the experience of minorities around the world in the past, and now, in the lives of those who live under corrupt governments and despotic regimes, etc.

39. Note: "Their rescue was not from subservience to independence, but from obligation to one lord to subservience to another, the Lord of heaven and earth" (Merrill, *Everlasting Dominion*, 330).

40. See Alexander, *Paradise*, 209.

41. Plato argued that being good brings individual happiness and social order.

42. Kaiser, *Ethics*, 83–84.

also a refraining from a contrary mode of action. . . . Consequently, when an evil is forbidden in one of the commands, its opposite good must be practiced before one can be called obedient."[43] Note next that recent research by psychologists has revealed that people often respond more effectively to negative sanctions than to promises of reward.[44] Finally, the way Deuteronomy handles the Ten Words makes it clear that the words stated as negative minimums (in Hebrew, e.g., "No murder!") imply positive maximums (the duty to do many positives).[45] So, by stating the commands in negative form God both increases the likelihood that we will obey and instructs us in our obligations to love God and our neighbor. Much good judgment comes from bad experiences; why not trust God's word and skip right to the good?

Perspectives on Biblical Law

Despite these considerations modern people react negatively to the Torah laws, like children being told they cannot eat all the candy they want. But note: the Mosaic law often represents accommodation to human sinfulness rather than God's ideals. Divorce (Deut 24:1–4) is as example. Jesus shocked his contemporaries by saying, "Because of your hardness of heart Moses allowed you to divorce your wives, but from the beginning it was not so" (Matt 19:8). Slavery fits this category[46] as does polygamy. That means that the Mosaic law about these things was intended to mitigate the worst behavior of sinful people, not teach God's desires. Much of the Mosaic Law is this way because the *nature* of law everywhere and always is to concern itself with regulating conditions in which things have gone wrong; otherwise, few laws would be necessary![47] The Torah contained the civil law of real people who often went wrong.[48] Discussion of the ethical issues legitimately raised

43. Kaiser, *Ethics*, 83.

44. "Penalties are usually more effective than rewards at spurring students and workers to improve." See John Tierney and Roy F. Baumeister, "For the New Year, Say No to Negativity," *Wall Street Journal*, December 27, 2019. See https://www.wsj.com/articles/for-the-new-year-say-no-to-negativity-11577464413 accessed 2–28–2020.

45. On the negative minimums implying positive maximums see Hopkins, "Understanding," 41–58, esp. 48–55: Deuteronomy's expositions of the Ten Words provide numerous examples of both prohibitions and positive obligations. Also Kaiser, *Theology*, 114–15.

46. Many ancient Jews saw it this way: see Daube, "Concessions," 1–13, esp. 3–5.

47. See the discussion of Matthew 19:8 in France, *Matthew* and that on Mark 10:5 in Lane, *Mark*. France thus comments that the place to get ethical principles is not from legal texts but from first principles in Genesis.

48. The Mosaic laws were for a theocracy, a government in which God is king and the people share a common faith. But the Torah instituted theocracy precisely to prove

by the Mosaic regulations is beyond the scope of this book but is treated in a wide literature.[49]

Modern Westerners are surprised that religion has often not demanded moral uprightness. This is because their experience is with Judaism and Christianity which do. In the Torah moral failure turned away God's favor. This was radical indeed! Even if one does not agree with all the moral specifics in the Torah, the expectation of conformity to moral standards should be appreciated rather than scorned.

Exodus 25–40: Building a House to Live Together

God's Presence

Leithart observes, "Now that Yahweh and Israel are married, Yahweh decides to move in with his bride. Most of the rest of Exodus is about the kind of house He wants Israel to build for Him (Exodus 25–40)."[50] It is dedicated to instructions for building the tabernacle, Israel's house, the place of God's presence among his people (Exod 29:42–45; 33:14). The furniture described here is the furniture of ancient homes.[51] For Israel, God's presence was the most prized of all things![52] The theme animates virtually everything in the book, but is especially prominent in God's revelation of himself to Moses (chapters 3–4), to Israel (chs. 19, 20, 24) and again to Moses (chs. 32–34). Exodus ends with God moving into his earthly home: his presence is concrete and permanent (Exod 40: 34–35).

---

its unsuitability for sinful people: God dispersed Israel for its failure, as Moses foresaw (Deut 31:24–29)! The Mosaic code *does not* justify its laws in today's different societies.

49. For example, Kaiser, *Ethics*; Copan, *Moral Monster*; Cowles et al., *No Mercy*. On slavery, Stuart, *Exodus*, 474–76, 278–80. On *lex talionis*, "law of retaliation" or "eye for an eye," (Exod 21:24–25) see Kaiser, *Ethics*, 101–5. Laws do not exist to encourage people to take vengeance: people are quite capable of this apart from any law! They exist to curtail and limit that natural human impulse! *Lex talionis* was a rule for judges, not for angry individuals (Exod 21:22). The rule is intended to limit the penalty to fit the crime and not go grossly beyond it.

50. Leithart, *House*, 79.

51. For a major study of God's presence see Duvall and Hays, *God's Relational Presence*.

52. Cole, *Exodus*, 40.

The Symbolism of the Tabernacle

Exodus 25–40 seems as tedious to modern readers as watching a TV program in a foreign language. The point is to show how God can dwell with Israel, but our problem is that we don't see that the language is symbolism. Dillard and Longman show that the location, design, and materials of the tabernacle are all symbolic![53] We must also note that Exodus employs more than one metaphor for the relationship of God and his people, which becomes clearer in Exodus 25–40. While the tabernacle is the house where God dwells with his bride, the relationship of God with his people is not identical with a marriage but is multifaceted. The location of the tabernacle at the center of Israel's encampment shows it is also the residence of Israel's king. Further, numerous elements make it clear that Israel's God is holy and so must be approached with proper preparation.[54] The design is likewise symbolic.

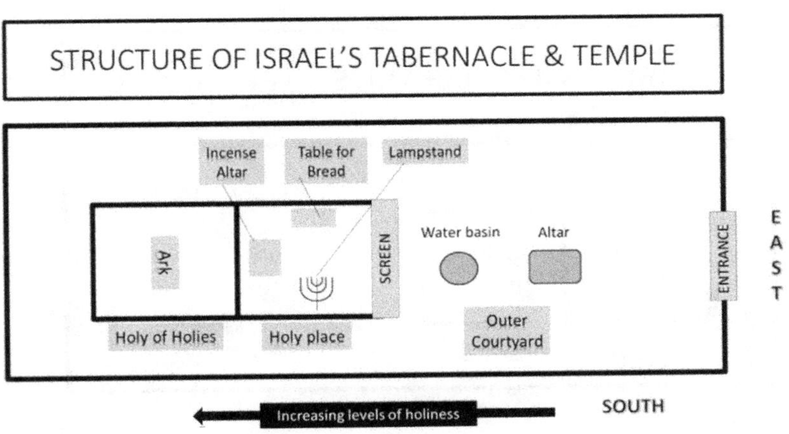

The three parts of the tabernacle (and later Israel's temple) represent varying degrees of holiness. The "Holy of Holies" is the holiest, since that is where God's presence dwells. Only the High Priest could enter there once a year to atone for the nation's sins. The Holy Place was less holy and could be entered only by priests. The Outer Court was less holy and could be entered by any Israelite who was ceremonially clean, as the entire nation was by virtue of being God's people. The Israelite camp itself was the least holy.

53. Dillard and Longman, *Introduction*, 68–71.

54. Holiness is a minor theme in Exodus but becomes a major one in Leviticus.

Outside the camp was the unclean Gentile realm. The camps of the Levites encircled the tabernacle to prevent the Israelites from getting too close to God's presence except when properly prepared. Uncleanness required temporary exit from the camp. One entered from the "east," which symbolizing uncleanness in Genesis after the fall.[55]

Beale points out that the tabernacle was a picture of the entire universe, as ANE peoples regularly viewed temples.[56] The Outer Court symbolized the world where people live, the Holy Place stood for the visible heavens and the Holy of Holiness represented the invisible realm where God lived. There is also symbolism in the priestly garments[57] and the echoes of Eden in the tabernacle.[58] "All of the flowers, angels, gold, and jewels call back to the garden of Eden, the place where God and humans lived together in intimacy. In other words, the Tabernacle is a portable Eden, so to speak, where God and Israel live together in peace."[59] There is more here, but this is enough to demonstrate that the detail here is all purposeful.

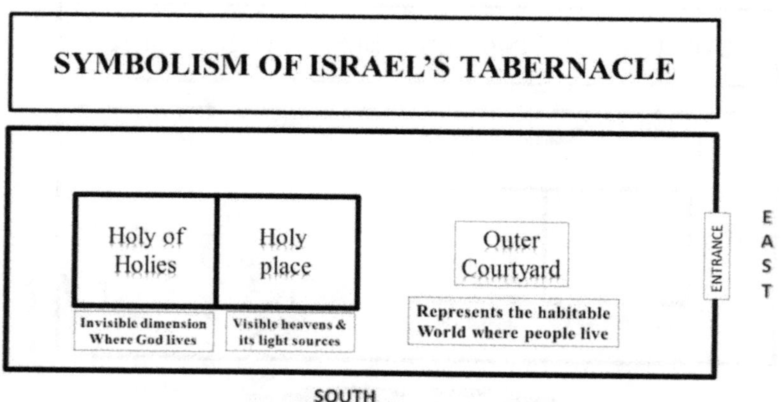

The tabernacle was God's house. The Psalmist cried out, "How lovely is your tabernacle, O LORD of hosts. . . . How happy are those who dwell in your house, ever praising you" (Psalm 84:1–4). Morales hits the nail on

55. Leithart, *House*, 82. See on "east" Gen 2:8; 3:24; 4:16; 11:2.

56. See Beale, *Temple*, and a more accessible presentation in Beale and Kim, *God Dwells Among Us*.

57. Beale, *Temple*, 40–41.

58. Leithart, *House*, 85. See also Morales, *Leviticus*, 96–98, 100–3.

59. Mackie, *Read Scripture*, 9. The Bible Project material is excellent. See also Beale and Kim, *God Dwells*.

the head stating the value of this material for the believer. It is "a tour of God's house."[60] It was constructed carefully according to a pattern shown to Moses (Exod 25:40), apparently as a copy of the heavenly reality of God's dwelling place. To walk through it and to perceive its symbolism is "a taste of heaven."[61] The descriptions here serve like the descriptions of the boundaries of the promised land before Israel arrived there (Num 34:1–15): to stir Israel's longing for a land beyond their current wilderness home. Believers of all times live in a wilderness, and the detailed descriptions of the New Jerusalem in Revelation 21:9—22:5 fan the believer's hope of a "better city" (Heb 11:16). The tabernacle serves to "convey the blessed lot of the redeemed who will find themselves abundantly satisfied with the fatness of God's house (Ps 36:8)."[62] Since most Israelites only saw the Outer Court, the descriptions allowed vision in the mind's eye.

The symbolism of the tabernacle (and the later temple) clearly resonate in the New Testament. Jesus was called Immanuel," "God with us" (Matt 1:23), showing that the presence of God is now among God's people in a more wonderful way than was ever possible in the Old Testament. Further, the NT says of Jesus (in Greek), "The Word became flesh and *tabernacled* among us" (John 1:18). The presence of God that was once limited to the tabernacle came among us to be seen, touched, and heard openly! In fact, Christians are now the "temple" of God individually (1 Cor 6:19) and corporately (2 Cor 6:16), since God's presence is with us permanently! What a privilege Christians have in experiencing the presence of God that OT saints could only taste at a great distance! But the final stage of this journey will be when God dwells among his people forever in the New Earth (Rev 21:3)!

THE MESSAGE OF EXODUS

The message of Exodus: The presence of God is the source of abundant life. To restore that life to people who have turned away from him, God reveals his character in the story of how he liberates people from bondage and declares good principles that promote life and blessing. Having thus introduced himself to allow us to get acquainted with him, God invites us to trust him and commit ourselves to him in a relationship akin to marriage. Saying "I do!" joins us with him in a committed relationship so that he can live with us and his presence can bring us abundant life and blessing.

60. Morales, *Leviticus*, 94. This discussion is indebted to Morales, 94–95.
61. Morales, *Leviticus*, 94.
62. Morales, *Leviticus*, 94.

Exodus one-sentence summary: To restore abundant life, God initiated a plan like marriage, in which he courted a people, invited them to commit themselves to him, and when they said, "I do," built a house so he could live with his people.

Exodus brief summary: God invites people into a committed relationship.

The brief take-away from Exodus: knowing God deeply and personally comes from experiencing his salvation and living close to him by trusting him and obeying his wise rules.

WHERE WE SEE JESUS IN EXODUS

Fretheim helps us see Jesus in Exodus.[63] Jesus, like Israel, and the Christian, is "called out of Egypt" (Matt 2:15; Hos 11:1) and tempted in the wilderness (Matt 4:1–11). Herod's murder of the children (Matt 2:16–18; Jer 31:15) echoes Pharaoh (Exod 1:15–22) and ungodly leaders through history. Jesus is the "supernatural rock" who followed Israel in the wilderness (1 Cor 10:4; Exod 17:6). He is a new Moses teaching his disciples from the mountain (Matt 5–7).

MEDITATING ON TORAH DAY AND NIGHT

Here are some key texts from Exodus for meditating on Torah day and night: Exodus 6:6–8; 9:3–15; 14:30–31; 15; 19:3–8; 34:6–7.

63. Fretheim, "Exodus," 257–8. All the examples are cited from Fretheim.

Chapter 7

The Message of Leviticus: Living Happily Ever After

Leviticus Brief Summary: Living happily ever after in relationships takes work.

In the *Star Wars* saga, after Padme and Anakin married, they grew to know each other better. She knew there was a dark side to Anakin, being aware of the revenge he had taken on those who had killed his mother, but they were happy and in love. In *The Revenge of the Sith* (Episode III, 2005) when Padme became pregnant Anakin had dreams of her dying in childbirth. Desperate to save her from what he feared would come true, Anakin was tempted by the dark side when Darth Sidious promised him a way to save Padme's life. Would they grow closer together, go away together and raise their child? Or would he break her heart by turning to the dark side, forcing them apart?

After courtship and marriage, two people begin to live together. These elements of the analogy we explored in Exodus. But moving in together is not an end but a beginning! Living together is more complicated that one understands beforehand! Ask any married person! No matter how much two people love each other, the early years of marriage are an adjustment to living harmoniously with a partner. Each is surprised when they learn things that they did not know would disappoint or frustrate their spouse. Each also learns things that can help or hinder the relationship that only living together in intimate contact can reveal. Such is the romance of marriage! It is hard work *and* the richest relational gift God has given. But the early stages of marriage are when a couple really get to know each other well. Each must choose to pursue those things that will draw them closer together and deepen their intimacy, rather than engage in behaviors that will strain the relationship and distance them from each other.

Leviticus is about those "marital adjustments," that is, learning to establish long-term intimacy. Leviticus develops what it means to live in close contact with God, disclosing what pleases him and what does not. As in any relationship, such positives and negatives are central to flourishing intimacy. As before, we will analyze the structure, themes and message of Leviticus as steps toward establishing intimacy with God.[1] We will also see Jesus in the book.

THE STRUCTURE OF LEVITICUS

Leviticus is the Center of the Torah

Why is the Torah arranged in five distinct subsections? A series of parallels between the Torah units suggests that Leviticus is the center of the Torah:[2]

Genesis	20,512[3]
Exodus	16, 723
Leviticus	11,950
Numbers	16,368
Deuteronomy	14,294

Leder comments:[4] "In the concentric structure of the Pentateuch parallels between Exodus and Numbers suggests that they constitute a frame for Leviticus. Parallels between Genesis and Deuteronomy not only

1. Leviticus is not a popular Bible book! Jacob Milgrom is considered by many *the* expert on Leviticus, in part because of his 2,700-page commentary on the book in the Anchor Bible series and his fifty years of studying the book! He notes that "In contrast with the wealth of commentaries on every book of the Bible published in the last century, Leviticus was singularly barren." See his *Leviticus*, xii. He says that this neglect is common among both Christians and Jews.

2. Many have argued this: see Morales, *Leviticus*, 23–27.

3. For word counts: http://www.aishdas.org/toratemet/en_pamphlet9.html accessed 3-9-2020. See Morales, *Leviticus*, 24, who suggested this comparison to me.

4. Leder, *Waiting*, 34–35.

frame Exodus, Leviticus and Numbers thematically, they also provide the beginning and conclusion to the linear sequence of the entire Pentateuchal narrative. Thus, Genesis through Deuteronomy exhibits in ABCB'A' organizational format in which Deuteronomy returns to and complements the themes of Genesis, and Numbers returns to and complements the themes of Exodus. This leaves Leviticus occupying the narrative center of the Pentateuch, as illustrated in the chart below."

A. Genesis	Separation from nations/ blessing/ seeing the land/ descendants and the land		
B. Exodus		Israel's desert journeys/ apostasy and plagues/ Pharaoh and magicians/ first-born/Levites	
C. Leviticus			Sacrifices/ cleanliness/ holiness
B'. Numbers		Israel's desert journeys/ apostasy and plagues/ Pharaoh and magicians/ first-born/Levites	
A'. Deuteronomy	Separation from nations/ blessing/ seeing the land/ descendants and the land		

So, besides the formal correspondences, those in content are striking and so are clearly intentional. This chart shows that the entire Torah is arranged in a chiastic structure (ABCB'A'), a form of repetition common in ancient literature in which the center is often the core emphasis.[5] Note in the chart that there are amazing content parallels between Exodus and Numbers.[6] It will be shown later that Genesis and Deuteronomy correspond in a series of ways, but note one arresting feature: "Genesis and Deuteronomy both end with a patriarch (Jacob, Moses) blessing the 12 tribes before dying

5. See for example, Dorsey, *Structure*, 41.

6. Wenham, *Pentateuch*, 109 points out some of these, though Sailhamer's list is fuller.

outside the land."[7] All of this justifies Leder's conclusion that Leviticus is the center of the Torah and thus its core.

There is also a broader structure showing that Leviticus stands at the center of the Torah. Sailhamer has shown a stunning chiastic structure at the center of the Torah, running from Exodus 1 through Numbers 24.[8]

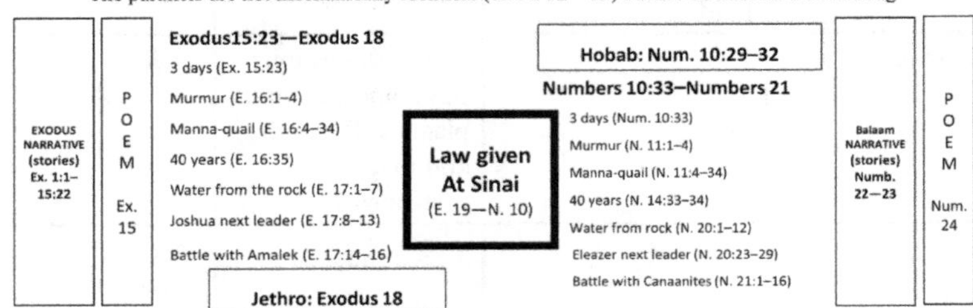

Several things are worthy of note. The center of the entire massive structure is the giving of the Mosaic Law at Mount Sinai, which constitutes Exodus 19 through Numbers 10 as a cohesive unit spanning three books in the Torah.[9] Note also the astonishing series of parallels that lead up to, then follow, the law-giving.[10] The point of these parallels is to mark the law-giving as the central focus. Also, the sheer volume of the material cannot be missed! It establishes the giving of the Law as the Torah's central focus.[11] Morales adds, "C. R. Smith also points out how the second half of Exodus deals primarily with setting up the Tabernacle, while the first half of Numbers is concerned with taking it down, Leviticus itself comprising God's

7. Morales, *Leviticus*, 24.

8. Sailhamer, *Meaning*, 366.

9. Recognition of Exodus 19:3–Numbers 10:10 as a unit is common: Sailhamer, *Meaning*, 366; Wenham, *Numbers*, 15–16; Wenham, *Pentateuch*, 104; Dorsey, *Structure*, 72. Multiple overlapping structures are common in the Bible.

10. Morales also notes these, *Leviticus*, 26, and cites others who have as well. I draw substantially in what follows from Morales's excellent work, *Who Shall Ascend the Mountain of the Lord?*

11. In an oral culture, bulk shows emphasis.

speeches from the tabernacle."[12] The conclusion is justified: the structure of the Torah shows that Leviticus is its center. This makes sense: weddings are nice, but marriage is the real deal and that means doing what will develop and deepen the love relationship, which is the preoccupation of Leviticus.

The Day of Atonement is the Center of Leviticus (and thus of the Torah)

We stated the broad structure of Leviticus earlier:[13]

1. Leviticus 1–7: Laws on sacrifice and the priesthood
2. Leviticus 8–10: Institution of the priesthood
3. Leviticus 11–16: Uncleanness and its treatment
4. Leviticus 17–27: Prescriptions for practical holiness

But this is only the content. The internal structure is more complex, as Morales shows:[14]

A. Lev 1–7	Sanctuary laws	Blood focus
B. Lev 8–10	Priestly laws	Blood focus
C. 11–15	Personal laws	Blood focus
D. Lev 16	Day of Atonement	Blood/Holiness focus
C`. Lev 17–20	Personal laws	Holiness
B`. Lev 21–22	Priestly laws	Holiness
A`. Lev 23–27	Sanctuary laws	Holiness

Morales argues persuasively for a chiastic structure with Leviticus 16 as the fulcrum around which the book pivots.[15] He sees a seven-part arrangement in which what leads to the Day of Atonement and what follows it mirror each other. The first three sections focus on blood, symbolizing life atoned for. The second group of three focus on holiness. This conclusion is supported by the most obvious feature of the book. Leviticus is utterly unique in being arranged as a series of thirty-seven speeches by God! Ross

12. Morales, *Leviticus*, 27.

13. Wenham, Pentateuch, 81–82.

14. Morales, *Leviticus*, 29, who cites numerous others who see the structure similarly.

15. Morales, *Leviticus*, 32, says seeing Leviticus 16 as the center of the book is "perhaps the widest consensus."

points out that this makes it "direct revelation more than the other books of the Pentateuch. . . . The bulk of the book consists of divine speeches.[16] Morales notes that this unparalleled structure makes Leviticus 16 "the literary center, with eighteen divine speeches on either side."[17] So, the Day of Atonement is the center of Leviticus.

Since Leviticus is the center of the Torah and Leviticus 16 is the center of Leviticus, this makes Leviticus 16 the central passage in the structure of the entire Torah! This is like putting the Day of Atonement in neon lights. The significance of this will be developed shortly.

THE THEMES OF LEVITICUS

Abundant Life

We have seen that the theme of Genesis is finding life from God and that of Exodus is getting to know God deeply and personally, all of which parallels courtship, marriage, and beginning to live together. Morales states how Leviticus continues this theme: "The primary theme and theology of Leviticus (and of the Pentateuch as a whole) is YHWH's opening a way for humanity to dwell in the divine Presence."[18] Ross agrees: the main concerns of the book—as well as of the Bible as a whole—are how God's people were supposed to order their lives now that the holy God dwelled with them and how they could maintain a relationship with him so that they could enter his presence to worship him.[19] Leviticus is concerned with the route to abundant life in a love relationship with God.

This concern with rich life is abundantly on display throughout the Torah. Wenham provides an example in his comments on Numbers 8:1–4. The passage deals with the golden lampstand, a seven-branched flowering tree in the tabernacle's holy place that symbolized the life-giving power of God. He states that often in Numbers the connections that an observant reader would notice are not explicitly stated. He explains:

16. Ross, *Holiness*, 16.

17. Morales, *Leviticus*, 28.

18. Morales, *Leviticus*, 23, emphasis in original. "YHWH" is how God's name is actually written in Hebrew, which was written without the vowels. With the vowels God's name is spelled "Yahweh" (mistranslated as "Jehovah" in the King James Version in 1611).

19. Ross, *Leviticus*, 20.

> Aaron is so to position the seven oil lamps placed at the end of each branch of the lampstand that they *give light . . . in front of the lampstand* (2–3). . . .The meaning of this action becomes apparent when the design of the holy place is taken into account. If the light beamed forwards it would have fallen on the table of shewbread, where 12 loaves of bread, symbolizing the 12 tribes of Israel, were heaped up (Lev 24:6–9). . . . This arrangement portrayed visually God's intention that his people should live continually in his presence and enjoy the blessing mediated by his priests.[20]

Morales explains how the structure of Leviticus speaks to this central theme:[21] "The first half deals primarily with the approach to God through blood, while the second half is taken up with life in God's Presence through increasing holiness, the overall goal being fellowship and union with God." Morales summarizes all this well: "As the innermost aim of the covenant, dwelling with God in the house of God, for fullness of life in abundant joy and fellowship, is the great promise held out before God's people."[22]

This is also the goal toward which all biblical revelation leads. Revelation 21:3–4 says, "And I heard a loud voice from the throne saying, 'Behold, the dwelling place of God is with man. He will dwell with them, and they will be his people, and God himself will be with them as their God. He will wipe away every tear from their eyes, and death shall be no more . . . for the former things have passed away.'" The goal of human relationships, especially marriage, is deep connection, a sense of meaning and belonging in being loved, joy instead of loneliness. God gave us the capacity for human relationships so that we could experience the joy and satisfaction they bring. But he created us for a deeper experience of which human relationships can only give a taste, the banquet of a relationship with him. This is the heart of Leviticus.

Life vs. Death

The opposite of life is death. To depart from God is to enter the realm of death. Both are major themes in Genesis and Deuteronomy (see below), and both are important in Leviticus. Both sin and uncleanness[23] tend toward

20. Wenham, *Numbers*, 94–95.

21. Morales, *Leviticus*, 29–30.

22. Morales, *Leviticus*, 18.

23. For discussion of "clean" and "unclean" in Leviticus see Alexander, *Paradise*, 260–6.

death. As Alexander says, "Only by becoming holy can a human escape the domain of death and experience the life-giving power of God."[24] Hence Leviticus must detail how people who have sinned (Lev 1–7) or become unclean (Lev 11–15) may remedy that situation so they can return to fellowship with God and thus enjoy his blessings. Since sin is very serious to a holy God, and since approaching God unprepared leads to death (Lev 10), Leviticus explains how to approach God safely. The core of that approach is through shed blood, which symbolizes life, which is accomplished through an animal substitute.

Holiness and Atonement

Holiness is the central theme of Leviticus. Its basic meaning is to be set apart from other things.[25] Regarding God it means he is completely good, separated from our sins. Due to our sins, we are as welcome in God's presence as an NRA advocate at the Democratic National Convention! Sin must be addressed before approaching God. This is Leviticus's aim.

Alexander explains that holiness also means "wholeness or perfection. To be holy is to be unblemished or unmarred. It is to experience life in all its fullness as God had originally intended it to be."[26] So, Morales is perceptive when he writes, "it is preferable to discern holiness not as an end in itself but rather as a means to an end, which is the real theme, the abundant life of joy with God in the house of God."[27]

But holiness is not just stopping sinful behavior. The stain of past sins must be addressed. Just as saying, "I'm sorry" is not enough to compensate for, say, robbing and beating someone, God justice demands appropriate redress to be made for our offenses against him and others. Leviticus says that payment can be made for our sins that satisfies a holy God's just penalty

24. Alexander, *Paradise*, 245.

25. There are holy garments in the OT (Exod 29:29). They are not "righteous," but "set apart" from mundane use for use only in the tabernacle by the priests. There are also "holy prostitutes" (Gen 38: 21), i.e., prostitutes who were devoted only to such work in a temple, not brothels. Gen 38 plays on the normal Hebrew term for "prostitute" (38:15) and the word sometime translated "cult prostitute" (38:21), which is simply a feminine form of the word "holy." Judah's friend wanted to dignify the illicit liaison somewhat by suggesting the act had been religious. Further, since sex was sometimes part of ANE worship, God went out of his way in the OT laws to separate anything that had anything to do with sex from worship. This is one reason menstruation, sexual intercourse, etc., made people unclean, which excluded them for a time from worship. These were not sins but ritual conditions.

26. Alexander, *Paradise*, 244. Wenham, *Leviticus*, 23–25

27. Morales, *Leviticus*, 30.

for them. The Bible term for payment is atonement. Instead of the sinner's death, in the Old Testament God accepted a substitute, the forfeiting of an innocent animal life, to satisfy God's justice (Lev 17:11).[28] The New Testament will provide a better substitute in the death of God's son, Jesus Christ, in our place. His voluntary death as an innocent satisfied all God's demands.

Leviticus 1–16 depicts all of this in a surprising way! In its successive sections, the reader "is placed in a position analogous to the high priest on the day of atonement, following in the path of holiness through the courtyard, holy place and holy of holies to the center of the book."[29] So, these chapters constitute a tour of the tabernacle, ending with the Day of Atonement (ch. 16), in which atonement is made in the Holy of Holies. The Day of Atonement is the heart of what atonement means and how it is achieved. In fact, "it was precisely the cultic [religious rituals] foundation for these theological categories that enabled the apostles of the new covenant to understand the accomplished work of Jesus Christ."[30] Once atonement has been made, ongoing holiness must be learned. This is the preoccupation of Leviticus 17–27.

Holiness can be graphed this way:[31]

Holy	Clean	Unclean
God alone is holy and he makes things and people holy	The normal state of most people and things	When sin makes unclean sacrifice restores a clean state

These distinctions also correspond to the Israelite camp.[32] The tabernacle is holy. Israel's camp surrounds the tabernacle and it is clean. Finally, outside of Israel's camp is the unclean realm of the Gentiles.

Morales clarifies the logic of the structure of Leviticus.[33] At the end of Exodus God takes up residence among his people (40:34–38), raising the question, "how may we approach the holy God who lives among us?" Leviticus 1–7 answers this by treating sacrifice. Then chapters 8–10 report the installation of the priesthood, those who mediate between a holy God and Israel by offering sacrifices. Next follows the story of Nadab and Abihu, two priests who were killed by divine judgment for offending God's holiness (Lev

28. Harrison, *Leviticus*, 31–32.

29. Morales, *Leviticus*, 32.

30. Morales, *Leviticus*, 30, note 28.

31. See Wenham, *Leviticus*, 18–25; Alexander, *Paradise*, 237–48.

32. See Alexander, *Paradise*, 239–41. The chart is drawn from Alexander, 240.

33. What follows is drawn from Morales's treatment in his excellent book *Leviticus*, 145–52.

10:1–3). What is then surprising is that the narrative ending with chapter 10 is interrupted until it resumes in 16:1. Why are chapters 11–15 inserted between chapters 10 and 16? The answer is that Leviticus 10:10–11 establishes the plan for the rest of the book. "You are to distinguish between the holy and the common, and between the unclean and the clean." Chapters 11–15 teach Israel how to distinguish the clean from the unclean so that the sin of Nadab and Abihu can be avoided. Next, chapters 17–27 instruct them in distinguishing between the holy and the common, or profane. Obeying this instruction they approach a holy God safely and receive rich blessing.[34]

To summarize, Leviticus 1–16 explains how to approach God: the divinely ordained way is through sacrifice (chs. 1–7) mediated by the priesthood (chs. 8–10), but this required the worshipper to be clean, so chapters 11–27 clarify cleanliness and holiness.[35]

Sacrifice

Sacrifice is the route to atonement.[36] It cleanses from sin and brings forgiveness (e.g., 4:20). Thereby the relationship between God and the Israelite, established by covenant but disrupted by sin, is restored. Sacrifice is an act of obedience recognizing that one deserves punishment for offending God's holiness. It demonstrates faith in God's merciful way to restore friendship. Faith is the root, obedience the fruit.

Atonement is a major theme of Leviticus,[37] indicating two major things. It means that a substitute has been made to spare the life of the offending party. It also means that a ransom has been paid, a just payment to buy the offending party out of debt for the offense.

Sacrifice also cost an Israelite something. In farming and herding economies animals were one's wealth. So, God demanded a form of sacrifice that required a (financial) sacrifice.[38] This reminded God's people that there was a cost to make things right, a lesson King David later embraced (2 Samuel 24:24). What we obtain too cheaply we esteem too lightly.

34. Morales, *Leviticus*, 150.

35. Milgram, *Leviticus* 1:768, says, "The explicit sources of impurity detailed in chaps. 11–15—carcasses, scale disease, genital discharges—together with corpses (Numbers 19) are all founded on this postulate: they symbolize the forces of death."

36. I follow here Wenham, *Leviticus*, 25–29. For a helpful treatment consult Alexander, *Paradise*, 249–59.

37. The Hebrew is *kipper*, from which is derived "Yom kippur," the Day of Atonement."

38. Harrison, *Leviticus*, 32.

Morales helpfully explains the way the sacrifices listed in Leviticus 1–7 normally worked for an individual who sinned in ancient Israel, as follows.[39]

1. *The presentation rite*: the worshipper presents the sacrificial animal to the priest who must verify that the animal meets the law's requirements. Compliance with the law demonstrates that the worshipper's heart is right toward God. As is typical in biblical narrative, the theology expressed in the sacrificial system "is not expressed in pronouncements but embedded in rituals."[40] Faith is the root, obedience the fruit.

2. *The hand-leaning rite*. The Hebrew says, "leaning heavily, or pressing down upon the animal with the hand," not "laying a hand" on the animal. The significance seems not to be transferring one's sins to the animal (it is to be blameless) but designating it as a vicarious ('in-one's-place") substitute. The animal will die in the worshipper's place.

3. *The slaughter rite*. The worshipper cuts the throat of the sacrificial animal, signifying that the worshipper submits to God's just judgment of his sins.

4. *The blood-manipulation rite*. According to Lev 17:11, blood symbolizes life. The priest was to sprinkle, splash, etc. (depending on the specific sacrifice) the blood on a sacred object in the tabernacle to pay the price of sin by forfeiting life so that the worshipper could be forgiven.

5. *The burning rite*. After the blood is manipulated, the animal (part or whole, depending on the sacrifice) is burned. This fire transforms the animal into a "pleasing aroma" that ascends to God. This symbolizes the worshipper's life being offered up to God and his acknowledging God's ownership of his life. It does *not* signify that God needs to eat, as many ancient Near Eastern religions believed (Psalm 50:9–13).

6. *The communion rite*. "Upon ascending into the heavenly abode of God, the Israelite enjoys the hospitality of the house of God."[41] While the offerings vary, in the peace offering the worshipper is given a portion of the sacrificial animal to eat with his family and friends in the presence of God. The meal symbolizes renewed fellowship with God. This clearly reminds the Christian of the Lord's Table, in which a meal symbolizes fellowship with God and his people.

39. Morales, *Leviticus*, 122–40. The sacrifices in Leviticus 1–7 are listed in a logical order, not in the order in which they were normally performed.

40. Milgrom, *Leviticus 1–16*, 42.

41. Morales, *Leviticus*, 137.

God's Presence

God's presence is a central theme of Leviticus.[42] God moved into his temple-house at the end of Exodus, and Leviticus is engaged with describing the implications of God's living among his people. Adam had access to God's presence in the Garden in Genesis, but his expulsion put a barrier between God and people.[43] Thereafter, approaching God was dangerous because he is holy while we are not. So, the question became, "Who shall ascend the mountain of the LORD? Who shall stand in his holy place?" (Psalm 24:3).[44] God is the source of abundant life! Leviticus is occupied with explaining how humans may approach God safely and so reengage his presence and his blessing. That is, Leviticus is concerned with regaining Adam's privilege and returning us to Eden—as much as is possible in a sinful world.

Leviticus 17–27 turns out "to possess the weightiest drama, and to hold out the most intimate manner of life in the divine Presence possible"[45] because it provides for a gradually deepening relationship with God: living happily ever after.

The key movement is in Leviticus 17–25, where the "tabernacle" becomes "the tent of meeting." Through weekly Sabbaths, the annual Day of Atonement and the annual festivals, the tabernacle becomes the place where Israel meets with God for fellowship and grows in holiness.[46] Thus "the unfulfilled purpose for which the cosmos was created [meeting with God as Adam and Eve had] may now be realized through the tabernacle cultus of Israel."[47]

Morales builds a convincing case that Leviticus 24:1–9 is the high-point of Leviticus 17–27.[48] It speaks of the lampstand in the Holy Place casting its light "continually" (used four times) upon the twelve loaves of bread symbolizing Israel (24:1–9).

42. See Wenham, *Leviticus*, 16–18; also Harrison, *Leviticus*, 30.

43. Morales, *Leviticus*, 55.

44. The Lord's residence is often pictured as a mountain.

45. Morales, *Leviticus*, 186.

46. Morales argues this in *Leviticus*, 194–203. This movement from "tabernacle" to "tent of meeting" is observable in the Hebrew terminology used in the Exodus tabernacle instructions (Morales, 195): "tabernacle" is used exclusively in Exod 25:9–27:19, while Exod 27:20–33:7 changes to the exclusive use of "tent of meeting."

47. Morales, *Leviticus*, 200.

48. Morales, *Leviticus*, 190–2.

Another feature that highlights the centrality of God's presence in Leviticus is that the book contains three theophanies (appearances of God), one in each part of the tabernacle.[49]

Section	Leviticus 1–10	Leviticus 11–16	Leviticus 17–27
Theophany	9:23–24	16:2	24:1–9
Occasion	Taber. inauguration	Day of atonement	Every weekly Sabbath
Place	Tabernacle court	Holy of Holies	The Holy Place
Audience	All Israel, once	High priest annually	Israel, perpetually, symbolized by God's light shining on twelve loaves

Themes Developed from Genesis

Leviticus is deeply rooted in Genesis. Morales argues convincingly that Genesis narrates a theme of growing alienation from God and his house[50] that Exodus begins to address and Leviticus remedies.[51] Leviticus's use of this material reinforces the Leviticus theme: the Lord has created a way for humans to dwell safely in his presence. We will treat a small number of these echoes of Genesis to validate the richness of the biblical use of previous material.[52]

One echo that Morales develops was touched on earlier: ANE people saw the cosmos as a temple-house for the gods.[53] "The cosmos was understood as a large temple and the temple as a small cosmos."[54] The creation story pictures God building himself a house (the universe), and the tabernacle accounts draw parallels between these two houses. For example, the

49. Morales, *Leviticus*, 204–5.

50. According to von Rad, *Genesis*, 152, the sin in Eden, the flood, and the Tower of Babel represent "an increase in sin to avalanche proportions."

51. Regarding Genesis see Morales, *Leviticus*, 39–74; regarding Exodus, see 75–107.

52. Scholars call this "intertextuality." Later texts pick up earlier texts and develop them. Since the original audience was illiterate and *heard* the text read out loud, repeating vocabulary and other similarities was the way biblical writers clued the audience that they were drawing from a familiar earlier theme. The authors assumed the audience would pick up on this and so felt no need to call attention to it as a modern writer would. Scholars often call these "echoes." Echoes are pervasive in the Old and New Testaments and add substantially to the depth and fascination of the biblical literature.

53. See Exod 23:19. Morales, *Leviticus*, 40–42; I draw from 39–74 in what follows. See also Beale, *Temple*.

54. Morales, *Leviticus*, 40.

"spirit of God" was present for the construction of the world (Gen 1:2) and the tabernacle (Exodus 31:3; 35:31). The term used for the lights God created in Genesis 1:14–15 is used elsewhere in the Torah *only* referring to the lamps in the tabernacle (e.g., Exod 27:20). Further, the seven-day creation account appears to be mirrored in the seven divine speeches about the tabernacle (Exodus 25–31), and the seventh day of creation is echoed in the seventh Exodus speech (Exod 31:2–17). The term translated "seasons" in Gen 1:14 *never* means the seasons of the year but instead refers to (usually) the "tent of *meeting*" or a "fixed time" for a cultic festival, or the festival itself.[55] "Eden's eastward orientation corresponds to the eastward entrance of the tabernacle."[56] Finally, the completion of the tabernacle in Exodus 39–40 echoes the completion of creation in Genesis 1:31—2:3.

This shows that the tabernacle in Exodus was described to echo creation and the garden of Eden. That is, the cosmos is a large temple (tabernacle) and the temple is a small cosmos. Thus, the high priest in the tabernacle who comes into the presence of God in the Most Holy Place is seen as an Adam figure, who does what Adam did when he walked with God in the Garden of Eden. In fact, the term for God "walking to and fro" in the Garden (Gen, 3:8) is also used for God's presence in the tabernacle (e.g., Lev 26:12).[57] So, the tabernacle is something of a replica of Eden, intended to reenact what Adam and Eve found there: communion with God! The tabernacle is the house of God, as was Eden.[58] The tabernacle and its sacrifices are a way to (partially) reverse the expulsion caused by sin and to return, as much as we can in a world of sin, to Eden, to God's presence.[59] Morales is spot-on: Leviticus, the Torah, and "all of the drama of Scripture is found in relation to this singular point of focus: *YHWH's opening up the way for humanity to dwell in his Presence once more.*"[60] This is how to live happily ever after.

THE MESSAGE OF LEVITICUS

The message of Leviticus: God wants to dwell with his people in love and intimacy but because he is holy and his bride is not, he establishes both procedures for approaching him in holiness and mediators to stand between himself and

55. Morales, *Leviticus*, 44.
56. Morales, *Leviticus*, 52.
57. Wenham, *Genesis,* 1:76; Morales, *Leviticus*, 52.
58. Morales, *Leviticus*, 53.
59. See Morales, *Leviticus*, 51–54.
60. Morales, *Leviticus*, 54, emphasis in original.

his people. These allow atonement to be made for sin so that God and his people can live together in harmony and joy. He then provides procedures for his people to maintain holiness to enable them to live happily ever after with him, and to please him expressing his holiness toward others by loving their neighbor as themselves (Lev 19:18).

Leviticus one-sentence summary: Since living happily ever after involves many adjustments, God established a plan to create and maintain intimacy with his bride by making her holy so they could share abundant life: a holy God can only be approached by holy people.

Leviticus brief summary: Living happily ever after in relationships takes work.

WHERE WE SEE JESUS IN LEVITICUS

We will briefly highlight a few ways Christians see Jesus in Leviticus. Alexander says, "The New Testament writers frequently understand the death of Jesus in sacrificial terms. . . . For the author of Hebrews, Jesus' death was the ultimate sacrifice, of which the Old Testament sacrifices were merely an illustration (9:9–10; 10:1).[61] Learning about these sacrifices helps to understand Jesus' sacrificial work.

Jesus is the high priest of which all Old Testament priests were mere shadows. He is superior to them because he was sinless. He is also from a different order of priests than the compromised priesthood of Aaron. He was "designated by God a high priest after the order of Melchizedek" (Hebrews 5:10; 7:11–22).

Jesus is the scapegoat that the Levitical one only symbolized. The OT goat bore the sins of Israel and carried them far away (Lev 16:21–22). This is what John meant when he said of Jesus, "Behold the lamb of God who *takes away* the sins of the world" (John 1:29).[62]

All that the Torah sacrificial system taught is fulfilled in Jesus.[63] Since only blood, that is, the sacrifice of an innocent life, can pay the price of God's outraged justice at our rebellions (Lev 17:11), Jesus the sinless one (Heb 4:15) gave his blood in death to pay the price God justly demanded (Hebrews 9:26). The price that we could not pay was paid by Jesus; that is, was paid by God to himself in the person of his son (Mark 10:45). Since we could not bear the punishment of our sins, Jesus acted the part of the scapegoat

61. Alexander, *Paradise*, 258.

62. See Alexander, *Paradise*, 256–7.

63. For a detailed theological analysis of Jesus' atoning work see Bird, *Evangelical Theology*, 385–434.

and bore our sins away (Lev 16:21; Isaiah 53:4, 12; 1 Peter 2:24). When a sin offering is made, forgiveness can be granted (Lev 4:26). All of this means that Jesus died as our substitute. So, God's righteous demands are satisfied (Romans 3:25; 1 John 2: this is the meaning of "propitiation")[64]. Forgiveness is offered to whoever believes God (Gen 15:6), which now means to trust in what Jesus did for them on the cross as sufficient to satisfy God (John 3:16). By that faith, Jesus' death is counted as covering one's debt (Ephesians 2:8–9; Romans 4:4–5). Stated differently, Jesus bore our sins. He became responsible for them on the cross. He stood in our place in God's sight. "For our sake he made him to be sin who knew no sin, so that in him we might become the righteousness of God" (2 Corinthians 5:21). God poured all his just wrath on Jesus instead of on us. Since the price God demands for sin is death (Gen 2:17; Rom 6:23), Jesus had to die under the onslaught of God's judgment. But then God raised him from the dead, showing that our sins are no longer standing between Jesus and God, because God's judgment has been satisfied. If God is satisfied against us because of what Jesus did, we can be satisfied and rest there as well. Each one who is satisfied with Jesus' work is declared a child of God (John 1:12).

MEDITATING ON TORAH DAY AND NIGHT

Leviticus 10:3; 10:10; 17:11.

64. See Bird, *Evangelical Theology*, 406–7 for elaboration.

Chapter 8

The Message of Numbers: Remaining Faithful Over the Long Haul

Numbers Brief Summary: Relationships require faithfulness grounded in trust.

The love story of Padme Amidala and Anakin Skywalker started beautifully but ended in heartbreak. Padme truly, deeply, loved him, as he loved her. But when he faced losing her as he had lost his mother, Anakin faced a choice. Would he be loyal to Padme and her wish for him to live with her whatever came? Or would he switch his allegiance to the dark side hoping to save her life that he feared would end in childbirth? When Padme confronted him and begged him not to devote himself to the dark side, Anakin chose poorly. In his anger, reflecting his dark side, he strangled her because he believed she had betrayed him. He abandoned his loyalty to her, giving in to the dark side, and she died as a result. The conflict in him boiled over into rage and he turned against her. Sadly, while he abandoned the better angels of his nature and went over to the dark side in order to save her, his new powers from the dark side were not able to save her, and he lost her anyway. His internal struggles led him to desert his first loyalty for one that failed him. Turning from his first loyalty ended in agony, not living happily ever after.

Relationships, including marriage, are like that over the long haul. As one becomes used to being married, it is easy to begin to take each other for granted, to focus more on the other's weaknesses than their strengths.

Inevitably spouses eventually face temptations regarding faithfulness. There are others who seem more attractive and less difficult that the one you have come to know so well! The old saying that "familiarity breeds contempt" describes too many married couples. This is one reason that marriages that start with love sometimes fail.

Like marriage, a believer's relationship with God also faces temptation. Following the Lord is sometimes difficult. Goals and attitudes other than those God commands beckon, and forbidden fruit can seem delightfully desirable. Two paths: which to choose? Over the long haul, believers must choose to remain faithful to God, to make him their first loyalty. That is the only path to living happily ever after with the Lord. This is the story of Numbers. By setting this choice before us in Numbers, God is preparing us for what he has prepared for us.

WHO WANTS TO READ A BOOK CALLED "NUMBERS"?

Who wants to read a book called "numbers"? It sounds like math, which scares many people more than snakes! But note that "Numbers" is not the original name and misrepresents the book's content.[1] The title always used by the Jews comes from the first Hebrew word of the book, *bemidbar*, which translates as "in the wilderness." That title is more appropriate to the book's content and has the added advantage that it doesn't scare off people who struggle with algebra or geometry! In fact, "wilderness" is a major biblical theme, because of how it appears in Exodus and Numbers, which will be discussed later. If we can set aside our initial negative response to this mistitled book, great lessons are to be found. The purpose of this chapter is to orient you to the book in such a way that you want to read it! Mission Impossible? Let's see!

THE STRUCTURE OF NUMBERS

Olson has pointed out that "A major obstacle to the appreciation and interpretation of any literary work is a perceived lack of coherence or organization. If no structure is detected, the work collapses into a jumble of unrelated fragments with no unifying purpose or meaning."[2]

1. The name "Numbers" comes from the Greek Septuagint translation (about 250 BC) of Numbers 1:2, "Take a sum of all the congregation of Israel . . . according to their *number*."

2. Olson, *Death*, 1.

Approaching a Bible book is like this. When one begins reading, it seems like reading the dictionary: each small unit is coherent, but there seems no connection to what comes before and after. But it turns out that reading the Bible is not like reading a dictionary. If one sticks with it, connections and continuities begin to emerge. Coherence slowly arises out of those "random statements." Structure materializes! Familiarity breeds recognition and comprehension![3]

Still, of all the Torah books, Numbers is the one which has been the hardest for readers to figure out. Even scholars who write books about Numbers have long been perplexed about its structure.[4] One survey of forty-six commentaries discovered twenty-four substantially different outlines for the book![5] This is partly because the variety of types of material in the book (narrative, poetry, lists, etc.) "surpasses that of any other book of the Bible."[6] The most common ways of organizing the book are by the chronological or geographic markers that punctuate the book, but "none of these schemes are persuasive."[7] In this case it would be understandable if people felt about Bible scholars the way they sometimes feel about economists: if you put all of them end to end, they would point in every conceivable direction.

The result? Numbers has not been the biggest Bible box office attraction! Duguid reports that when he told an OT professor that he was preaching through Numbers, the scholar commented that he thought that the book was hardly meant to be preached![8] Failure to find a framework is the fundamental fault. This could change if a coherent structure cracked open the book's meaning. Fortunately, someone has finally done just that! Dennis Olson has established that there is a clear plan to the book. Because his detailed argument is such a breakthrough, we will rely heavily upon his work here.[9]

The basic structure of Numbers is two-part:[10]

1. Numbers 1–25: The Old Generation of Rebellion
2. Numbers 26–36: The New Generation of Hope

3. An excellent resource is DeRouchie's *Understand*.

4. Wenham, *Pentateuch*, 103, speaks for the majority, scholars and laymen alike, when he says, "It is not clear exactly how it should be divided."

5. Olson, *Death*, 31.

6. Milgrom, *Numbers*, xiii.

7. Dillard and Longman, *Introduction*, 86.

8. Duguid, *Numbers*, 13.

9. Olson's 1985 *Death*, his doctoral dissertation at Yale, is the primary study. His *Numbers* (1996) is more accessible.

10. Olson, *Numbers*, 5–6.

Several things justify this structure. The most eye-catching feature of Numbers is its two long lists that occupy Numbers 1 and 26. Olson argues that the lists constitute the primary structural device of Numbers, dividing it into two sections which contrast two generations in Israel. The old generation is those who left Egypt and saw the plagues and crossed the sea with Moses. They eventually died in the wilderness due to unbelief and rebellion against God. The new generation is their children, who were not unbelieving, and who would eventually inherit the promised land. Olson's book title summarizes the contrast: *The Death of the Old and the Birth of the New*. He affirms, "the structure and symmetry of the two census lists in chapters 1 and 26 provide further formal evidence that they operate as the introduction of the two halves of the book."[11] By this contrast, God previews what awaits every generation believers. God is preparing us for what he has prepared for us. Here is a partial list of the symmetries between the two halves.[12]

Numbers 1–25	Numbers 26–36
Old Generation of Rebellion	New Generation of Hope
1–census of twelve tribes	26–census of twelve tribes
3–census of the Levites	26–census of the Levites
5–legal discourse involving women	27–legal discourse involving women
9–Passover celebration	28:16–25–Future Passover instructions
13–list of 12 spies who spied out the land	34–list of 12 leaders to divide the land
13–14–the story of the spies	32:6–15–spy story retold to new generation
21:21–35–victory over Sihon and Og	32–assignment of lands of Sihon and Og
25–Midianite opposition and curse	31–Midianite curse fulfilled

These parallels are dazzling! The two halves are artfully crafted to show the similarities between the older generation and their children. But the purpose of that comparison is to prepare the reader to also be struck by the jarring *contrast* between the two generations, which is more important. The grand contrast comes at the end of each half, when one dies in the wilderness, while the other is poised in hope at the edge of the promised land. The book is about what caused that distinction, and what lessons these two generations hold for all generations of God's people.

The first half of the book divides into two parts. Numbers 1–10 recounts the preparation for the march to the promised land, where Israel will

11. Olson, *Death*, 87.

12. See the full list in Olson, *Numbers*, 5–6. The list here is slightly adapted.

inherit God's grand promise and its rich blessing. The future looks bright! The substance is "the ordering of God's people according to the commands of the LORD and their faithful obedience to those commands."[13] But a startling and surprising change occurs in 11:1: "And the people complained in the hearing of the LORD about their misfortunes." The substance of Numbers 11–36 is foreshadowed in that opening statement! As Olson paints it, "While 1:1—10:36 is a completely positive picture of the relationship with God and his people, 11:1—25:18 is overwhelmingly dominated by a series of rebellions and plagues and death with periodic glimmers of hope but ultimate failure."[14]

The second section of part one (11:1—25:18) begins with six incidents of rebellion in rapid succession (11:1—20:29). But one has a hopeful unit (15:1–36) in the middle recounting regulations that assume an ultimate inheriting of their land.[15] Each section contains death or a threat of death. The last one is the ultimate tragedy: the public disobedience of the leaders when Moses strikes the rock (20:1–21), which concludes with the death of Aaron (20:22–29).[16]

The last unit of part one consists of two episodes of God blessing Israel with victories (21:1–2; 21:10–25), each followed by rebellion and death (21:4–9; 25:1–18). But embedded in this section is the intriguing story of Balaam (22:1—24:25).[17]

A king named Balak is frightened of Israel and hopes for divine intervention to defeat Israel by paying a prophet to curse them. The gist of this complex and circuitous story is that in spite of Israel's near-constant faithlessness to God, God is loyal to them and refuses to allow a curse to be pronounced upon his people.[18] Here is the key signal of hope in the midst of a section largely preoccupied with the unbelief and disobedience of God's people.

Olson detects three passages in Numbers that announce the book's theme directly: 14:20–37, 26:63–65, and 32:6–13.[19] The first census was at Sinai in Numbers 1. Chapter 26:63–65, which ends the second census of the new generation in Moab, is representative. "These were those listed by Moses and Eleazar the priest, who listed the people of Israel in the plains of

13. Olson, *Death*, 122.

14. Olson, *Death*, 122.

15. Olson, *Death*, 119.

16. Olson, *Death*, 119.

17. Olson, *Death*, 119–20.

18. Olson, *Death*, 95.

19. Olson, *Death*, 90–93.

Moab by the Jordan at Jericho. But among these there was not one of those listed by Moses and Aaron the priest, who had listed the people of Israel in the wilderness of Sinai. For the LORD had said of them, 'They shall die in the wilderness.' Not one of them was left, except Caleb the son of Jephunneh and Joshua the son of Nun." The text encapsulates the book's theme: a new generation has risen (26:63) who is not condemned to death (26:64–65): *the death of the old and the birth of the new*. God is preparing us for what he has prepared for us.

The second section of Numbers (26–36) is a remarkable antithesis to the first one. The second census is taken not in the wilderness but on its edge, the entry point to Canaan in the plains of Moab, striking a hopeful tone: the wilderness wanderings are now past. Olson conveys the essence of the section: "Following the census in Numbers 26, the second half is bracketed by an inclusio in chapters 27 and 36. Both of these chapters relate a legal dispute involving the daughters of Zelophehad and the inheritance of property and thereby frame the second half of Numbers. The legal issue involving land is resolved in both cases . . . In contrast to the deaths of a whole generation in a series of rebellions and judgments in the first half of Numbers, the second half does not record the death of any Israelite."[20]

An important note is struck by the way the book is structured. Numbers (and the Torah) does not end with this second generation *entering* the land promised by God. Instead, it ends with them poised for the conquest, but with the end not yet determined. The third theme text (Numbers 32:14–15), where God speaks to the second generation, is instructive: "And behold, you have risen in your fathers' place, a brood of sinful men, to increase still more the fierce anger of the LORD against Israel! For if you turn away from following him, he will again abandon them in the wilderness, and you will destroy all this people." The point is not that they are predestined to do better than their parents, but that they *may* do better, if they believe and obey.

To summarize, Numbers is structured to draw a contrast between one generation who died in the wilderness due to unbelief and rebellion, and another generation who had the opportunity to choose a different path. In other words, when temptation came the first generation was unfaithful to the Lord. Would the second be faithful over the long haul? God is preparing us, the readers, for what he has prepared for us.

20. Olson, *Numbers*, 6–7.

THE THEMES OF NUMBERS

In a sense, the major theme of Numbers is now seen to be a reiteration of one that we have seen before: choosing life instead of death by choosing faith and obedience. Faith is the root, faithfulness the fruit. But there are also other major themes.

Parallels with Exodus

We showed earlier that the Torah's five books center on Leviticus, with Exodus and Numbers framing it, and Genesis and Deuteronomy framing the entire Torah.[21] We need to revisit our observation that Exodus and Numbers share parallel content in order to show how the argument of the Torah has developed since then. Wenham lists some of those parallels.[22]

Miriam's Song of Praise	Exodus 15:20–21	Miriam and Aaron rebel	Numbers 12
Three-day trip to Sinan	Exodus 15:22	Three-day trip from Sinai	Numbers 10:33
Complaint about water	Exodus 15:22–26	Complaint	Numbers 11:1–3
Manna and quail	Exodus 16	Manna and quail	Numbers 11:14–25, 31–35
Water from rock	Exodus 17:1–7	Water from rock	Numbers 20:1–13
Advice to Moses from father-in-law	Exodus 18:1	Advice to Moses from father-in-law	Numbers 10:29
Leaders to assist Moses	Exodus 18	Leaders to assist Moses	Numbers 11:16–30
Israel defeats Amalek	Exodus 17:8–16	Israel defeated by Amalek	Numbers 14:39–45

Wenham then astutely observes: "Clearly readers are expected both to remember the earlier incidents in Exodus as they read Numbers and to compare them. It is quite obvious in several of these incidents that things have deteriorated from Exodus to Numbers."[23] He goes on to mention Miriam's about-face and the reversal of fortune with Amalek. He also calls attention to God's changed response to complaints that bring manna and quail: in

21. See our explanation of the structure of Leviticus in chapter 7.

22. Wenham, *Pentateuch*, 109, slightly adapted. Sailhamer, *Meaning*, 366 is fuller.

23. Wenham, *Pentateuch*, 109.

Exodus God graciously provides, whereas in Numbers he sends a plague among them to punish their attitude.[24] Alexander points out another parallel: "Various episodes in Numbers closely parallel Exodus 15:22—17:16, where the theme of 'testing' is prominent. . . . Although the concept of testing is mentioned only once in Numbers, it is clear from the material in Exodus that, although God intended the desert experience to test the faith and obedience of the Israelites . . . it was they who tested God."[25]

The ultimate parallel is that Exodus and Numbers each narrate a disastrous crisis that hails from unbelief. In Exodus 32–34 it is the golden calf betrayal. In Numbers 13–14 it is the faith-failure at Kadesh-barnea in which Israel refuses to enter the promised land due to fear. In both cases God threatens to destroy the nation and to create a new nation beginning with Moses, and Moses' pleading with God averts that disaster.[26] But while the two episodes are clearly parallel, the Numbers breach of faith is worse. The result of the golden calf is the death of some in the camp, but God still commands them to continue their journey to the promised land (Exod 32:34). Numbers is very different: God condemns that entire generation to death by wandering in the wilderness (Num 14:32–35), and the journey to the land is halted in its tracks (Numbers 14:39–45). Again, a delivery like a brick through a plate-glass window. It is too bad that generation didn't know Booker T. Washington's advice: "associate yourself with people of good quality, for it is better to be alone than in bad company." Israel chose the bad company of the spies who said conquest was impossible rather than the good company of Joshua and Caleb who said that trust in a good God would bring good results.

The point of Moses composing the two books so that their parallels are noticed is to drive home the message that the nation has deteriorated. Despite God bringing them out of Egypt and showing them continual goodness and mercy, Numbers is showing that as time passes, Israel is proving unfaithful to their God. People can choose trust and faithfulness, or they can choose the opposite. The first generation chose poorly. Like trying to put toothpaste back into the tube, some actions cannot be undone. They must now do without the indispensable: God's favor. Nonetheless, God favors them repeatedly in his mercy until they all die in the wilderness.

24. Wenham, *Pentateuch*, 110.

25. Alexander, *Paradise*, 276, 279.

26. Wenham, *Pentateuch*, 110–11.

God's Presence

Morales recognized that "Exodus, Leviticus and Numbers each has the ascent into God's Presence at the center (Exod 19; Lev 16; Num 17)."[27] Exodus 19 begins the central unit of the book as the people come before God at Mount Sinai to enter into his covenant. Leviticus 16 describes the Day of Atonement, when the high priest enters the holy of holies annually for the nation. Morales is also correct about Numbers 17 being at the center of that book. Numbers 13–14 narrate the paramount crisis of the book at Kadesh-barnea, while chapters 16–17 dissect that unbelief by rehearsing three further episodes of unbelief and rebellion. In Numbers 17 God meets Moses in the tent of meeting and makes Aaron's staff of dead wood blossom in a life-out-of-death symbol of what his presence does, especially as Israel draws close to God through Aaron's priesthood and the tabernacle sacrifices.[28] These three incidents stress that the presence of God among his people is of paramount importance, and that his presence is the source of life.

The pillar of cloud over the tabernacle is a symbol of God's presence like the Royal Standard flag over Buckingham Palace signals the queen's presence. It is interesting that while the cloud is absent in Genesis and rarely appears in Deuteronomy (five times) and Leviticus (two times), it is mentioned exactly twenty times in both Exodus and Numbers, highlighting both the parallel nature of the books and the importance of God's presence in them.

Yet there is a terrible irony in Numbers regarding God's presence. Soon after Israel refuses to enter the Land at Kadesh-barnea, Numbers recounts the story of Korah's rebellion. Numbers 16:1–6 obviously parallels the story of Nadab and Abihu in Leviticus 10:1–3. In both cases men took censers and put fire in them and incense on them as an offering to the Lord. The problem was that *only* those designated by God may do this. Nadab and Abihu died instantly because they presumed to enter God's holy presence without authorization. But in Numbers 16:3 a man named Korah argues that "all in the congregation are holy, every one of them," implying that Aaron should not have special privileges as a priest when all the people of Israel were holy. He was claiming that God's holiness did not require priests to stand between God and the holy people; God's presence should be equally accessible to all Israelites. As a response, God had Korah and his company do what Nadab and Abihu had done (16:6), and the result was the same: death (16:31–35). Here is the irony that emerges when Kadesh-barnea and

27. Morales, *Leviticus*, 221, note 2.

28. Morales, *Leviticus*, 221.

Korah's rebellion are placed back to back: "the Israelites were too fearful to enter the land of Canaan . . . yet they had no fear of YHWH himself. Indeed, because Israel did not fear YHWH they would fear their enemies."[29] Israel fails to recognize that the presence of God is the greatest possible treasure, yet it is also brings great responsibility to treat a holy God with respect and approach him only by the means he has revealed. Otherwise, his presence brings death. The "divine Presence has escalated the prospect for Israel, either for abundant life or judgment and death."[30]

Life vs. Death

We have already seen that life and death are themes in Numbers. We should reiterate here that the grand story dealing with death is Kadesh-barnea, where that entire generation that refused the land is condemned to die in the wilderness (Num 13–14). But chapters 16–17 record three other incidents, most already treated, which each involve life and death (16:1–35; 16:36–50; 17:1–13). At the center of Numbers this Genesis theme is rewritten in bold print.

Faith and Obedience

The primary lesson about faith in Numbers is about Israel refusing to enter the land at Kadesh-barnea (Num 13–14). The terrible results are a perennial lesson for believers. But Numbers has another lesson. It is the story of two generations of Israel journeying through the wilderness toward Canaan, showing that the believer's life in every generation is extending God's kingdom through struggle. Merrill explains the two aspects of this well:

> As man was placed in the Garden of Eden to keep and rule it, so Israel would be placed in Canaan to keep and rule it as a fiefdom from the Great King. . . . Israel's occupation of Canaan, then, is to be seen as a stage in this process of claiming all creation for the Creator. . . . Israel had to understand that occupation of the land could be achieved only through much travail, for Canaan, like creation itself, was under alien domination and it had to be wrested away by force, by the strong arm of Yahweh, who would fight on behalf of his people.[31]

29. Morales, *Leviticus*, 222.
30. Morales, *Leviticus*, 222.
31. Merrill, *Biblical Theology*, 60.

Duguid calls this "living between salvation accomplished and salvation consummated." For Israel this was "between the exodus and the Promised Land." He continues, "We live as they did—between salvation accomplished and salvation completed. We live between the work of God in accomplishing our salvation at the cross and the time when that salvation will be brought to its consummation when Christ returns. . . . our experience of this world is likewise one of wilderness rather than fullness."[32] These stories are examples for us in faith and obedience (1 Cor 10:6). Merrill declares, "The journey itself is of theological significance for it serves paradigmatically as the experience of every pilgrim who makes his way from promise to possession."[33] By this lesson, God is preparing us for what he has prepared for us. The support promised for us is the same as then: God's presence (Matt 28:20).[34]

Wilderness

The wilderness is a prominent Torah theme that "reverberates throughout the Bible."[35] It denotes a place that is inhospitable to life, and it is the location of Israel from Exodus through Deuteronomy. The main Hebrew word for wilderness (Hebrew *midbar*) occurs 105 times in the Torah but is most prominent in Numbers.[36] It has two opposite associations there. It refers to a place of wandering, discipline by God, and death (esp. Numbers 14), where the term is more abundant than anywhere else in Scripture. But it is also a place where God provides what the environment cannot provide: water, food, clothing, etc.[37] Mercy even in discipline!

The wilderness symbolizes both danger and God's provision. The danger can be seen in two ways in Scripture. The first sign of this appears when Deut 32:10 refers to the wilderness as a waste, where the term "waste" repeats a key term from Genesis 1:2, translated there, "The earth was *without form*." The wilderness of Israel's wanderings is like an undoing of the creation, like the time before God made the earth a hospitable environment.[38] This image is reinforced when Numbers 32:13 declares that "the LORD's anger was kindled against Israel, and he made them *wander* in the wilderness forty

32. Duguid, *Numbers*, 18, 19, 19.

33. Merrill, *Biblical Theology*, 61.

34. Duguid, *Numbers*, 19.

35. Dillard and Longman, *Introduction*, 90.

36. Baker, "Wilderness," 893, 894; the term is used forty-eight times in Numbers.

37. Baker, "Wilderness," 897.

38. Baker, "Wilderness," 896.

years." The word "wander" is used only four times in the Torah, twice of Cain as a "fugitive" (ESV) on the earth after God disciplines him (Gen 4:12, 14), and here of Israel's wilderness wandering.[39] Here the fate of Israel after Kadesh-barnea is to walk the path of Cain, though God still provided for them (Deut 29:5) as he still cared for Cain (Gen 4:15). So, the wilderness is a place of danger and discipline. The New Testament picks up this wilderness image in Mark, where Mark frames his prologue with four uses of the term (Mark 1:3, 4, 12, 13). By this he depicts Jesus' life as a wilderness experience of opposition and danger from the beginning.[40] Again, the believing life is one including struggle, not only joy.

The wilderness as a place of God's provision is also a prominent theme. Hosea 2:14–15 sees the early period in the wilderness as the time when God wooed and loved Israel, "entering into a marriage contract with her," their "honeymoon."[41] God provided for his people in the wilderness as he later did for Jesus there (Mark 1:13). Waltke speaks well: "Lacking normal human structures of society and life and confronted with the hostility of the environment and enemies, Israel finds its life in God. They are learning to be in the world, but not of it. . . . the elect nation is taught in the wilderness to depend totally on God and his word."[42] By this instruction, God is preparing us for what he has prepared for us. We still need to learn that man does not live by bread alone, or money alone, or technology alone, but by every word that comes from the mouth of God.

Waiting for the Land

The classic film, Casablanca (1943), opens describing how desperate people tried to flee World War II Europe to the safety of America by making their way "cross the rim of Africa to Casablanca in French Morocco. Here the fortunate ones through money or influence or luck might obtain exit visas and scurry to Lisbon, and from Lisbon to the New World. But the others wait in Casablanca, and wait. . .and wait. . .and wait." It seems strange that beginning with God's promise to Abraham to give him a land (Gen 12:1–3), the entire Torah is an experience of "waiting for the Land."[43] Except for the grave he purchases, Abraham never inherits any of the land (note Hebrews

39. The other place is Exod 20:18, which is not directly related.

40. See Lane, *Mark*, on Mark 1:1–13.

41. Baker, "Wilderness," 897.

42. Waltke, *Theology*, 540.

43. The title of Leder's book is *Waiting for the Land*, which insightfully develops this theme throughout the Torah.

11:8–16). While the land is the grand experience of waiting, waiting is a defining experience throughout the Torah! God promises Abraham to make him into a great nation, but he chose to promise this to a barren couple (Gen 11:30; note the double affirmation of infertility emphasized in the text). That meant God built into their experience the necessity of waiting on him to bring about the impossible! And wait they did—for years—for that promise to be kept. Waiting is one of the key tensions in the Abraham stories. Joseph also waited, through no fault of his own, for years for God to make clear why he allowed the surprising and seemingly pointless suffering Joseph endured—until the fog finally lifted and Joseph saw through new eyes that God "doeth all things well" (Gen 45:8; 50:20). So, waiting is a major component of the spiritual life and Numbers is a prime source of this theme. Wenham affirms, "The whole book of Numbers looks forward to the occupation of the land of Canaan. Chapters 1–10 describe the preparation for the journey from Sinai to Canaan, 11–12 the journey itself, 13–14 the abortive attempt at conquest. The rest of the book describes the subsequent period of wanderings and their period of waiting in Transjordan prior to their entry."[44] These are more than historical facts about God's promises to ancient Israel. They are seen in the New Testament as foreshadowing distant future realties that apply to all of God's people. Hebrews 11:14–16 refers to God's promise of the land to Abraham: "For people who speak thus make it clear that they are seeking a homeland. . . . But as it is, they desire a better country, that is, a heavenly one." It seems appropriate therefore to hold that the Torah's story of exodus, journey in the wilderness and waiting for the land are a picture of the life of every believer, and that they provide lessons for that spiritual journey. Olson is thus justified in applying Numbers to all believers: "the new generation in the second half of Numbers functions as a paradigm for every succeeding generation of God's people. . . . The concern of the book is to establish a model or paradigm which will invite every generation to put itself in the place of the new generation."[45] Leder, in his fine examination of the waiting theme in the Torah, rightfully draws the lesson from this theme: "As a whole, then, the Pentateuch declares to God's people of every generation that the presence of God *already is*, but that the land is *not yet*, a present reality. Until the exile is completely resolved by the coming again of Immanuel, God's people will have no place to call home."[46] Israel's experience is ours, as Waltke suggests: "Instead of living in the rich land of milk and honey, the Israelite wanderers find themselves unexpectedly in

44. Wenham, *Numbers*, 43.

45. Olson, *Death*, 183.

46. Leder. *Waiting*, 196.

barrenness, living in tents and staggering between oases."[47] By teaching us to wait, God is preparing us for what he has prepared for us. Contemporary Christians also struggle, but in hope for the future, and sustained by God's presence, which is our treasure (1 Timothy 6:17–19). When that future arrives, believers will be as at home as Harry Potter at Hogwarts.

Remaining Faithful Over the Long Haul

So, the grand lesson of Numbers is that believers must choose trust and obedience over fear, doubt and disobedience. The first generation out of Egypt, who saw God's miraculous plagues on that country, and who saw God humble the mightiest monarch on earth nevertheless cowered in fear before the rag-tag armies of Canaan, fearing man more than God. They failed to remember that with faith nothing is impossible but without faith, nothing is your reward. Their unbelief and disobedience lead to death. All believers always live a wilderness experience, tested by circumstances we cannot control but attended by a God who promises to walk with us all the way. But we also have a promise of a land yet to come, just over the horizon. Two roads. Which to choose? That first generation chose poorly and died. The second would choose wisely and would inherit. In each generation, believers face the same choice. Will we remain faithful to our beloved Lord over the long haul?

THE MESSAGE OF NUMBERS

The message of Numbers: Believers who have seen the power and grace of God have every reason to trust and obey him, and may obey him for some time, but over the long haul, as fear and temptations arise, those who were faithful may choose to forget God's goodness and choose poorly, opting to believe what circumstances suggest, complaining because they cannot understand what God is doing, preferring present comfort to future blessing; or they may choose to trust God's promises and act in faith, fixing their hope on what God has promised them. One path leads to loss of blessing, conflict and ultimately death; the other leads to blessing, resolution of conflicts, hope and ultimately life.

Numbers one-sentence summary: Each generation of God's people must choose whether to remain faithful over the long haul, choosing unbelief and disobedience with the tendency toward death (loss of blessing), or faith and

47. Waltke, *Theology*, 540–1.

obedience with the tendency to enhance life (God's rich blessing). Numbers prepares us for what God has prepared for us.

Numbers brief summary: Relationships require faithfulness grounded in trust.

WHERE WE SEE JESUS IN NUMBERS

We have seen already that the wilderness is symbolic of the Christian life in several respects. This will be developed further later in the book. But we also see in Numbers that the priesthood stood as mediators between God and his people. Numbers 6:22–27 is one of the Torah's most beautiful texts. It reads:

> "The LORD spoke to Moses, saying, 'Speak to Aaron and his sons, saying, Thus you shall bless the people of Israel: you shall say to them,
> The LORD bless you and keep you;
> the LORD make his face to shine upon you and be gracious to you;
> the LORD lift up his countenance upon you and give you peace.'
>
> So, shall they put my name upon the people of Israel, and I will bless them."

Poythress well says that in giving this blessing regularly to Israel, "the priests serve as figures mediating between God and his people. They prefigure a final mediatorial figure who will have no need to offer sacrifices for His own sins, because He is the perfect Mediator."[48]

In 1 Corinthians 10:4–6 Paul declares, "For they drank from the spiritual Rock that followed them, and the Rock was Christ. Nevertheless, with most of them God was not pleased, for they were overthrown in the wilderness. Now these things took place as examples for us, that we might not desire evil as they did." Paul is referring to the two incidents in Exodus and Numbers where water came from the rock. He says that the Rock was Christ, because the one who provided Israel all she needed was the Lord Jesus Christ. Jesus was always the active presence of God with his people, and whenever we see God active for his people in the Old Testament, we see Jesus.

Alexander notes that Jesus' temptations in the gospels echo Israel's in Numbers. "Indeed, it is impossible to fully understand the story of Jesus temptations without appreciating how he is contrasted with the Israelites who came out of Egypt. Whereas the ancient Israelites were tested in the wilderness and failed, Jesus, as the new Israel, succeeds. This theme is

48. Poythress, *Shadow*, 52.

reflected all three temptations."[49] He says that Jesus and Israel both experienced hunger, a test about God's ability to save, and God's promise to grant a future kingdom. Jesus trusted and obeyed, as we should.

MEDITATING ON TORAH DAY AND NIGHT

Numbers 6:22–27; 14:7–9; 14:11; 20:11–12; 21:8–9; 23:19; 32:23.

49. Alexander, *Paradise*, 283.

Chapter 9

The Message of Deuteronomy: Choose Life!

By Derek Van Pelt Campbell, with George Van Pelt Campbell

Deuteronomy Brief Summary: Loving and obeying God is choosing life!

Over the course of the *Star Wars* saga many characters die in their fight to defeat the empire, or in their fight to defend and protect it. This has led to some memorable last lines from some of the characters that we have come to know and love. Padme says of her husband Anakin, "Obi-Wan, there is good in him. I know, I know there is, still."[1] Before his death, Yoda says, "Luke do not underestimate the powers of the Emperor, or suffer your father's fate, you will. Luke, when gone am I, the last of the Jedi will you be. The Force runs strong in your family. Pass on what you have learned. Luke, there is another Skywalker."[2] When Luke dies after a lightsaber duel with Kylo Ren, he simply says, "See you around, kid."[3] Last words have a way of sticking with us. We remember them. They define a story.

1 *Star Wars Episode III: Revenge of the Sith*. Directed by George Lucas. Lucasfilm Ltd, 2005.

2 *Star Wars Episode VI: Return of the Jedi*. Directed by George Lucas. Lucasfilm Ltd, 1983.

3 *Star Wars Episode VII: The Last Jedi*. Directed by Rian Johnson. Lucasfilm Ltd, 2017.

This is what we find when we turn to Deuteronomy. The book is Moses' last words to the people of Israel. Like Luke, Leia, Han and C-3PO, Moses has been a part of the story for a long time. We first meet him when he is called by God through a burning bush in Exodus. He travels to Egypt and tells Pharaoh to let God's people go. He walks with them through the Red Sea. In Leviticus, he gives the Israelites God's instructions about how an unholy people can approach a holy God. Then in Numbers, Moses journeys with them through the wilderness and brings the people to the border of the promised land. Moses has been with God's people for more than forty years. He is old and about to die. Before he does, he takes one more opportunity to remind the Israelites of who God is and who he has called them to be. Deuteronomy is Moses' last words to the people of Israel, and his final words are, "choose life!" (Deut 30:19–20).

THE STRUCTURE OF DEUTERONOMY

Moses' final words to the people in Deuteronomy are given in the form of a sermon. Moses delivers this sermon as the people stand on the border of the promised land. This sermon was delivered by Moses during the last few days of his life. Joshua picks up where Deuteronomy leaves off, with the people entering the promised land under their new leader Joshua.

Moses' sermon that makes up the bulk of Deuteronomy is not just one sermon, but actually three sermons. This shows us the first way to understand the structure of Deuteronomy. The book can be divided into a short introduction and then three sermons by Moses, followed by a conclusion. Accordingly, the book is broken down as follows:[4]

Introduction	Deuteronomy 1:1–4
Moses' first sermon	Deuteronomy 1:5—4:43
Moses' second sermon	Deuteronomy 5:1—29:1
Moses' third sermon	Deuteronomy 29:2—30:20
Conclusion	Deuteronomy 30:21—34:12

This structure helps us to understand the message of the book because each of the three sermons has a different focus and purpose. Moses is telling the people three different things in three different sermons and these three sermons, much like individual episodes in the *Star Wars* saga, build upon each other to form one continuous story. We can see this by looking at the

4 Block. *Deuteronomy*, 43–48.

content of the three sermons. Note that each section begins by calling attention to Moses' words.

Sermon	Passage	Topic	Opening Verse
Moses' first sermon	Deuteronomy 1:5—4:43	Moses reviews the history of how the Israelites came to the border of the promised land.	Deuteronomy 1:5: "Moses began to expound this Torah, saying . . ."
Moses' second sermon	Deuteronomy 5:1—29:1	Moses reviews the law given to the people at Mt. Sinai, God's instructions for how they should live.	Deuteronomy 5:1: "Moses summoned all Israel and said . . ."
Moses' third sermon	Deuteronomy 29:2—30:20	Moses encourages the people to obey and warns them of the consequences if they disobey.	Deuteronomy 29:2: "Moses summoned all the Israelites and said to them . . ."

There is a second way to understand the structure of Deuteronomy that comes to us from the study of ANE societies contemporary with Israel. Many societies at this time would make formal agreements using something called a suzerain-vassal treaty. This type of treaty was an agreement between the suzerain, the more powerful party and the vassal, the less powerful party. In these agreements, the suzerain agreed to the ways that he would care for and protect the vassal. The vassal agreed to the ways that he would serve the suzerain in thanks for his care and protection. Deuteronomy is written in the form of a suzerain-vassal treaty.[5] According to this understanding, the book would be broken down as follows[6]:

SV treaty section	SV treaty section contents	Corresponding Deut passage	Deuteronomy passage contents
Preamble	Introduces the suzerain and the vassal.	Deuteronomy 1:1–4	Introduces all the main characters and tells where and when the events take place.

5. This structure is widely acknowledged in contemporary scholarship See, for example Merrill, *Everlasting Dominion*, 327–30; Craigie, *Deuteronomy*, 20–24. See also Merrill, *Deuteronomy*, 29–47.

6. Merrill, *Deuteronomy*, 30–32. See also Kitchen, *Ancient Orient*, 90–102.

Historical prologue	Reviews the historical events that have led the suzerain and the vassal to form this treaty.	Deuteronomy 1:5—4:43	Moses reviews both God's and Israel's actions that have led to this point.
General stipula-tions	Outlines briefly what the suzerain requires.	Deuteronomy 5	States the Ten Words given at Sinai.
Specific stipula-tions	Outlines the vas-sal's obligations in detail.	Deuteronomy 6–25	Expounds each of the Ten Words in order, giving positive and negative examples.
Bless-ings and curses	Outlines the blessings and curses that will come from following or breaking the stipulations of the treaty.	Deuteronomy 26:1—28:68	Moses tells Israel what will hap-pen if they follow God's Torah and what will happen if they do not.
Suc-cession arrange-ments	Ratification cer-emony, calling of divine witnesses to the treaty and provision of regular public reading of it.	Deuteronomy 29:1—34:12	In Deut 29, Israel ratifies the covenant; Deut 30:19 calls the divine witnesses; Deut 31:9–13 provides for regular public reading of the Torah.

Understanding the book as three sermons and understanding it as a suzerain-vassal treaty are not mutually exclusive. In fact, these structures fit together well. Moses' first sermon corresponds to the historical prologue. Moses' second speech corresponds to the stipulations and blessings and curses. Moses' third speech and the conclusion correlate to the succession arrangements. Merrill sees Deuteronomy this way: the *Shema* (Deut 6:4–5) is the core, which the Ten Words elaborate, and the body of Deuteronomy expounds in detail.[7]

7. Merrill, *Everlasting Dominion*, 330; Merrill, *Deuteronomy*, 31.

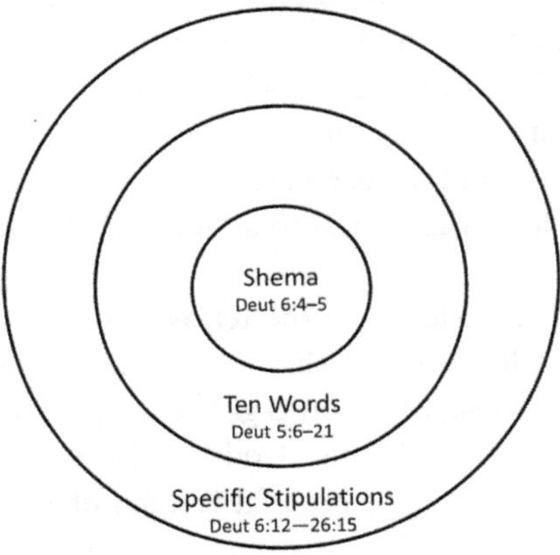

THE THEMES OF DEUTERONOMY

Love[8]

One of the things that sets Deuteronomy apart from other suzerain-vassal treaties of the same time period is the reason Israel, the vassal, is called to follow the instructions of God, the suzerain. Usually, these types of treaties were made because a people was conquered in warfare. The victorious king or nation often forced those conquered to sign the treaty against their will. They would also often impose strict duties on those they had conquered. Deuteronomy could not be more different. God makes a covenant with his people not because he has conquered them in warfare but because he loves them. The first main theme of Deuteronomy is that God loves his people and desires them to love him in return. God knows that if we love him, we will do for nothing what others will not do for anything.

We can see this by looking at the stipulations section that makes up the bulk of the book (chapters 5—26). Here Moses outlines God's instructions for how God's people should live. This large section starts with the Ten Words in Deuteronomy 5. Deuteronomy 4:13 says, "He proclaimed his covenant to you, which he ordered you to obey, the Ten Words; and he wrote them on two stone tablets" (CJB).[9] As we saw earlier, in the Jewish reckoning, the first of the Ten Words is, "I am the LORD your God, who

8. See, for example Alexander, *Paradise*, 290–293.

9. Taken from the *Complete Jewish Bible* by David H. Stern. Copyright © 1998. All rights reserved. Used by permission of Messianic Jewish Publishers, 6120 Day Long Lane, Clarksville, MD 21029. www.messianicjewish.net.

brought you out of Egypt, out of the land of slavery." God's Ten Words begin not as cumbersome commandments, but with a reminder of God's grace and love. Because God loves his people so much, he delivered them from slavery and set them free. The other nine words that follow show what our response should be to this loving, redeeming, slavery-defeating, setting-free God! They explain love: willingness to do for God for nothing what others will not do for anything.

We can see further evidence of the Ten Words as an expression of God's love and freedom by looking at their context. Before the giving of the Ten Words, Moses makes clear why God is giving the people these commands. In Deut 4:37, we are told, "Because God loved your ancestors and chose their descendants after them, he brought you out of Egypt by his presence and his great strength." God's love is given as the explicit reason for the prohibition against making images. Deuteronomy 5:8–10 says, "You shall not make for yourself an image in the form of anything . . . for I, the LORD your God, am a jealous God, punishing . . . those who hate me, but showing love to a thousand generations of those who love me and keep my commandments." Finally, we see that God gives his people these Ten Words because he loves them and desires good things for them. After Moses proclaims the Ten Words, he says in Deut 5:32–33, "So be careful to do what the LORD your God has commanded you. . . . Walk in obedience to all that the LORD your God has commanded you, so that you may live and prosper." God gives commands and instructions to his people not to be mean but because he loves us and desires the best for us.

Not only does God love us, but he desires that we love him. We see God's call for us to love him in Deut chapter 6, the chapter following the giving of the Ten Words. In Jewish tradition, Deut 6:4–5 are the most important verses in Deuteronomy, and in the entire Hebrew Bible. These verses are so important that they have a name, the *Shema*, which comes from the Hebrew word for "hear," the first word of these verses. These two verses sum up our call to love God in response to his love for us. The *Shema* says, "Hear, O Israel: The LORD our God, the LORD is one. Love the LORD your God with all your heart and with all your soul and with all your strength." God desires for us to love him in response to his love for us. Note that loving God bookends the main section of Deuteronomy (Deut 6:4–5; 30:20). By this we see the deepest motivation for obedience. God knows that people who love him will do for nothing what others will not do for anything.

Sometimes when people attempt to read Deuteronomy, they lose sight of God's love for us and our call to love him in the central section (Deuteronomy 5–26) because it contains much more legal material than the rest of the book. This section, though, is an extended teaching on what God's love looks like in practice.[10] After the Ten Words are given in Deut 5, Moses spends the next twenty-one chapters teaching and expanding on what the Ten Words mean, and how we can follow and apply them in everyday, real-life situations. The Ten Words expound the *Shema*. We see how the bulk of Deuteronomy expounds the Ten Words in the following chart:[11]

Word	Content	Exposition in Deuteronomy
1	Deut 5:6: "I am the LORD your God, who brought you out of Egypt."	Deuteronomy 6–11
2	Deut 5:7–10: "You shall have no other God's before me . . . but showing love to . . . those who love me and keep my commandments."	Deuteronomy 12
3	Deut 5:11: "You shall not misuse the name of the LORD your God, for the LORD will not hold anyone guiltless who misuses his name."	Deuteronomy 13:1—14:27
4	Deut 5:12–15: "Observe the Sabbath day by keeping it holy. . . . the LORD your God has commanded you to observe the Sabbath day."	Deuteronomy 14:28—16:17
5	Deut 5:16: "Honor your father and mother . . . so that you may live long and that it may go well with you."	Deuteronomy 16:18—18:22
6	Deut 5:17: "You shall not murder."	Deuteronomy 19:1—22:28
7	Deut 5:18: "You shall not commit adultery."	Deuteronomy 22:9—23:18
8	Deut 5:19: "You shall not steal."	Deuteronomy 23:19—24:7
9	Deut 5:20: "You shall not give false testimony against your neighbor."	Deuteronomy 24:8—25:4
10	Deut 5:21: "You shall not covet . . . [what] belongs to your neighbor."	Deuteronomy 25:5–16

Life and Death

One Sunday when I, Derek, was a young pastor, I was enthusiastically preaching my sermon when something happened that I did not expect. One of the members of the congregation, a small woman in her mid-eighties,

10. Merrill, *Deuteronomy*, 31.

11. Numerous scholars give similar but slightly different divisions of the units. The verses used here are by the author, George Campbell.

stood up right in the middle of my sermon and said in a loud voice, "Well pastor, what do you want me to do?" I honestly don't remember what Scripture I was preaching on that day or what the point of my message was. The only thing I remember is this woman standing up and asking, "Well Pastor, what do you want me to do?"

This is a good question, a question that we see reflected in Deuteronomy. As we have said, Deuteronomy is a series of three sermons that lead to a choice. Everything that Moses says in the Deuteronomy leads up to a call to action that we find near the end of the book. In what many people consider to be the theme verse of the entire book[12] Moses says to the people in Deut 30:19–20, "I have set before you life and death, blessings and curses. Now choose life, so that you and your children may live and that you may love the LORD your God, listen to his voice and hold fast to him. For the LORD is your life and he will give you many years in the land he swore to give to your fathers, Abraham, Isaac and Jacob." Moses has spent thirty chapters repeatedly encouraging the people to follow God's laws so that they might be blessed. Then, like the good preacher that he is, Moses ends with a call to action. Moses ends his sermon with a choice. No one has to interrupt Moses' sermon and ask, "Well Pastor, what do you want me to do?" Moses tells us what he wants us to do: choose life!

This choice between life and death forms a pair of bookends around the entire Torah. We see it at the very beginning of Genesis when God instructs Adam and Eve not to eat the fruit from the tree of the knowledge of good and evil. God instructs them what to do, but then he leaves the choice up to them. They can choose life or choose death. Sadly, Adam and Eve choose death. They choose not to follow God's instructions. At the very end of the Torah, we find the same choice. Moses has laid out God's instructions. He has told the Israelites what will happen if they obey and what will happen if they do not. Then, as with Adam and Eve, God leaves his people a choice. The choice between life and death has passed from just two people to the entire nation of Israel. Deuteronomy ends where Genesis began, with the choice to follow God and receive life, or to turn away from him and come to death. The second theme of Deuteronomy is the choice between life and death, and it is a choice that Moses shows us that all people must make. We each face the same choice as Adam and Eve, and Moses encourages us to choose life.

12. Block, *Deuteronomy*, 711.

Faith and Obedience

The third theme of Deuteronomy is faith and obedience. In order to choose life, we must live by faith so that we can obey God's instructions. This is clear from the beginning of the book. In the first chapter of Deuteronomy, Moses is recounting the story of the Exodus generation choosing not to enter the promised land. God had called them to enter the land, but the people were afraid because of the obstacles that they faced. Moses says (Deut 1:29–33), "Do not be terrified; do not be afraid of them. The LORD your God, who is going before you, will fight for you, as he did for you in Egypt. . . . you saw how the LORD your God carried you, as a father carries his son. . . . In spite of this, you did not trust in the LORD your God, who went ahead of you on your journey . . . to show you the way you should go." Notice what is happening here. Moses does not say, "You did not obey the LORD's commands." Moses does not say, "You did not listen to what God told you to do." Moses does not say, "You did not follow God's instructions." Moses says, "In spite of this, you did not *trust* the LORD your God." Moses knows that the people's disobedience results from lack of faith. They did not trust God to lead them.

At the end of Deuteronomy, we see again that following God's instructions is primarily a matter of faith. Obedience requires trust. In order to obey God's commands and decrees, we must have a changed heart, a heart that has learned to trust. In Deuteronomy 30:6, Moses says to the people that, "The LORD your God will circumcise your hearts and the hearts of your descendants, so that you may love him with all your heart and with all your soul and live." It is not a coincidence that two verses later, Moses says in Deut 30:8, "You will again obey the LORD and follow all his commands I am giving you today." Moses mentions obedience only after he has mentioned a changed heart. Obedience comes from faith, from a heart that has learned to trust. A few verses after that, Moses reminds the people once again that God is not asking them to live up to some impossible standard but calling them to trust in him for salvation. Deuteronomy 30:12–14 says, "Now what I am commanding you today is not too difficult for you or beyond your reach. It is not up in heaven, so that you have to ask, 'Who will ascend into heaven to get it and proclaim it to us so we may obey it?' . . . No, the word is very near you; it is in your mouth and in your heart so you may obey it." Obedience is a response to faith and trust. If the Torah was only about changed behavior, Moses would not say, "The word is very near you. It is in your mouth and in your heart." Moses knows that obedience begins in the heart. Moses is reminding the people that obedience to God's instruction is ultimately about having hearts that are changed by him, hearts that have learned to trust him. The point of Moses' sermon is to remind the people of

God's grace and provision so that they will trust in him. Moses knows that for the people to follow God's good instruction in the Torah, they must trust in him. Deuteronomy shows us that obedience flows from faith.

Meditating on Torah

In *Star Wars: Episode V Return of the Jedi*, Luke Skywalker has a vision in which he sees his friends suffering at the hands of Darth Vader. Luke makes the decision to leave before his Jedi training is complete, despite the protests of both Yoda and Obi-Wan Kenobi. As he is preparing to leave the planet Dagobah, Yoda offers one last piece of instruction. Yoda says, "Strong is Vader. Mind what you have learned. Save you it can."[13] While Yoda is speaking about Luke's training in the ways of the force, his words could just as easily apply to God's instruction in the Torah. "Mind what you have learned. Save you it can."

The fourth theme of the Deuteronomy is meditating on the Torah. Over and over, Moses encourages the people of Israel to remember God's instructions to them. He tells them to remember the example of the people who came before them who did not meditate on the Torah and the end to which that brought them. He tells them to remember the blessing and life that God has promised if they follow his ways. Moses encourages the people to always have God's instructions in the Torah front and center in their minds. In short, Deuteronomy is a series of sermons encouraging the people to meditate on the Torah day and night.

This is clear from how Joshua begins. Joshua 1:6–8 says, "Be strong and very courageous. Be careful to obey all the law my servant Moses gave you; do not turn from it to the right or to the left, that you may be successful wherever you go. Keep this Book of the Law always on your lips; meditate on it day and night, so that you may be careful to do everything written in it. Then you will be prosperous and successful." God commands Joshua to remember his instructions given through Moses. Do not forget them. Do not turn to the right or to the left. Keep God's instructions always on your lips. Meditate on them day and night. God's instructions to Joshua sound a lot like Yoda's instructions to Luke Skywalker, "Mind what you have learned. Save you it can." Remember that in the Jewish ordering of the Scriptures, Joshua is the first book of the Prophets. So, the Prophets start with a call to meditate on the Torah day and night. We see this again at the beginning of the Writings, the third section of the Hebrew Bible. The Writings start with

13 *Star Wars Episode V: The Empire Strikes Back*. Directed by Irvin Kershner. Lucasfilm Ltd, 1980 (Note: Future uses of this same quote will not be cited).

the Psalms. In Psalm 1:1–3 we read, "Blessed is the one . . . whose delight is in the law of the LORD and who meditates on his law day and night. That person is like a tree planted by streams of water, which yields its fruit in season and whose leaf does not wither — whatever they do prospers." Note the similarities between the opening of the Prophets with Joshua and the opening of the Writings with the Psalms. Both begin with a call to meditate on Torah day and night. Both also say directly that we should meditate on the Torah day and night so that we can prosper in all that we do. "Mind what you have learned. Save you it can."

We see this theme of meditating on Torah day and night made very clear in one of the most famous passages of Deuteronomy itself. The *Shema* in Deut 6 tells us, "Hear, O Israel: The LORD our God, the LORD is one. Love the LORD your God with all your heart and with all your soul and with all your strength. These commandments that I give you today are to be on your hearts. Impress them on your children. Talk about them when you sit at home and when you walk along the road, when you lie down and when you get up. Tie them as symbols on your hands and bind them on your foreheads. Write them on the doorframes of your houses and on your gates." This is a beautiful and lengthy description of what it means to meditate on Torah day and night. We see this same type of language repeated several times throughout Deuteronomy. We find it in Deut 4:9–10. In Deut 11:18–21, we find language almost identical to that we find in the *Shema*. Moses tells the people, "Fix these words of mine in your hearts and minds; tie them as symbols on your hands and bind them on your foreheads. Teach them to your children, talking about them when you sit at home and when you walk along the road, when you lie down and when you get up. Write them on the doorframes of your houses and on your gates, so that your days and the days of your children may be many in the land." Many times throughout the Deuteronomy, we find Moses encouraging the people to mediate on Torah day and night. In other words, "Mind what you have learned. Save you it can."

Care for the Weak and the Vulnerable

The final theme of Deuteronomy comes out of the ones before it. When we choose life in God through faith and obedience, we seek to grow in that faith and obedience through meditating on the Torah day and night. One of the main ways our lives show this is through care for the weak and the vulnerable. Care for the weak and the vulnerable is one of the outward expressions of the change that God works in our hearts through faith in him and by meditating on his word. A heart changed to love God should also be changed to love our neighbor, whom God also loves.

Throughout Deuteronomy the weak and the vulnerable are represented by three different groups of people: widows, orphans, and foreigners. These three groups are often mentioned together. They were the most weak and vulnerable to exploitation when Deuteronomy was written. Throughout Deuteronomy, we find Moses encouraging God's people to care for those who are weak or vulnerable. We see some examples of such instruction in the chart below.

Reference	Passage	Summary
Deuteronomy 1:16	"Hear the disputes between your people and judge fairly . . . [including]between an Israelite and a foreigner residing among you."	Justice should be administered fairly regardless of whether someone is an Israelite or not.
Deuteronomy 5:14–15	"Observe the Sabbath day by keeping it holy. . . . you shall not do any work, neither you . . . nor any foreigner residing in your towns. . . . Remember that you were slaves in Egypt."	Foreigners, as well as servants and animals, are included in God's command to celebrate the Sabbath and are equally entitled to God's rest.
Deuteronomy 10:18–19	"God defends the cause of the fatherless and the widow. He loves the foreigner residing among you, giving them food and clothing. You are to love those who are foreigners, for you yourselves were foreigners in Egypt."	God loves the weak and the vulnerable and we should as well. This reflects the heart of God.
Deuteronomy 14:28–29	"At the end of every three years, bring all the tithes [so that] the foreigners, the fatherless and the widows who live in your towns may eat and be satisfied and so that the LORD your God may bless you."	Israel was commanded to provide for the weak and the vulnerable.
Deuteronomy 16:11–12	"Rejoice before the LORD your God . . . you, your sons and . . . the foreigners, the fatherless and the widows living among you. Remember that you were slaves in Egypt."	The weak and the vulnerable were to be included in the joy and celebration of the Jewish feasts.

Deuteronomy 24:17–18	"Do not deprive the foreigner or the fatherless of justice, or take the cloak of a widow. . . . Remember that you were slaves in Egypt."	Do not deprive the weak and the vulnerable of justice.
Deuteronomy 24:19–22	"When you are harvesting in your field and overlook a sheaf. . . . Leave what remains for the foreigner, the fatherless and the widow. Remember that you were slaves in Egypt."	Israel was commanded to not deprive the weak and the vulnerable of justice and to go out of their way to provide for them.
Deuteronomy 27:19	"Cursed be anyone who withholds justice from the foreigner, the fatherless or the widow."	There are serious consequences for abusing the weak and vulnerable.
Deuteronomy 31:12	"Assemble the people . . . and the foreigners residing in your towns—so that they can listen and learn to fear the LORD your God."	The weak and the vulnerable were to be included in the regular public reading of the Torah.

One final thing to note about caring for the weak and the vulnerable is the reasons that God often gives for these commands. There are two reasons that occur multiple times throughout Deuteronomy. The Israelites are told to remember that they were slaves in Egypt and that God delivered them from there with a mighty hand. They are to care for the weak and the vulnerable because they remember that they, too, were weak and vulnerable. The other reason is so that God might bless them. They will receive God's blessing by treating the weak and the vulnerable with justice and showing them God's love. Those who love God will do for others for nothing what others will not do for anything.

THE MESSAGE OF DEUTERONOMY

The message of Deuteronomy: Because God loves us and desires for us to love him, he offers us a real choice between life and death. This is a choice that each one of us will have to make. Deuteronomy is comprised of three sermons in which Moses encourages us to choose life through faith in God. We grow in faith and obedience by meditating on the Torah day and night. One way that this faith and obedience to God's instructions shows itself in our lives is caring for the poor and the vulnerable.

Deuteronomy one-sentence summary: Deuteronomy is comprised of three sermons that Moses delivered shortly before his death in which he reminded the people of God's past faithfulness, reviewed God's instructions, and encouraged them to obey God's instructions so that they might be blessed with life.

Deuteronomy Brief Summary: Loving and obeying God is choosing life!

Key take away: God gives us his instructions not as some impossible standard, but because he loves us and desires the best for us. When we follow God's teaching and instruction, we are blessed with life in and through him.

Theme verse: Deuteronomy 30:19–20: "I have set before you life and death, blessings and curses. Now choose life, so that you and your children may live and that you may love the LORD your God, listen to his voice and hold fast to him. For the LORD is your life and he will give you many years in the land he swore to give to your fathers, Abraham, Isaac and Jacob."

FINDING JESUS IN DEUTERONOMY

Jesus Quotes Deuteronomy

When we look at the life and ministry of Jesus, it is clear that he viewed Deuteronomy as God's discipleship manual. Jesus had Deuteronomy, in Moses' words, "in his mouth and in his heart." We can see this by looking at how Jesus quotes and refers to the words of Deuteronomy throughout his life and ministry. In fact, Jesus quotes Deuteronomy more than any other book of the Old Testament.[14] We will look at five examples of important times he did so.

First, Jesus quotes Deuteronomy when he is facing temptation from the devil. He reflects on Deuteronomy and remembers the many ways that God the father was with his people. In the first temptation in Matthew's gospel, Satan tempts Jesus to turn the stones around him into bread because he has not eaten in forty days and is hungry. Jesus quotes Deut 8:3, saying, "Man shall not live on bread alone, but on every word that comes from the mouth of God." In the second temptation, Satan encourages Jesus to throw himself off the highest point of the temple to see if God will save him. Jesus responds with Deut 6:16, saying, "Do not put the LORD your God to the test." Finally, Satan tells Jesus that he will give him authority over all things if Jesus will only worship him. Jesus replies, quoting Deut 6:13, "Away from

14. Block, *Deuteronomy*, 26.

me, Satan! For it is written: 'Worship the LORD your God and serve him only.'" When Jesus faces temptation, he quotes only one book: Deuteronomy.

Next, when Jesus gives his most famous teaching, the Sermon on the Mount, he quotes Deuteronomy multiple times. We will look at just one example. In Matthew 5:21 Jesus says, "You have heard that it was said to the people long ago, 'You shall not murder.'" Jesus is quoting the Ten Words. Notice, though, that he does not just quote them. Instead, Jesus does three things. He affirms God's negative command, reinforcing the prohibition. Jesus also broadens the implications of the negative command. In Matthew 5:21–22, Jesus says, "You have heard that it was said to the people long ago, 'You shall not murder and anyone who murders will be subject to judgment.' But I tell you that anyone who is angry with a brother or sister will be subject to judgment." Notice that Jesus is saying that God is not only concerned about murder. If we are angry or say cruel things, that is the root which might give birth to murder! Last, Jesus gives the positive implication of the negative command. In Matthew 5:23–24, Jesus says, "Therefore, if you are offering your gift at the altar and there remember that your brother or sister has something against you, leave your gift there in front of the altar. First go and be reconciled to them; then come and offer your gift." Do you see how much is present in the simple command, "You shall not murder"? Jesus affirms the negative command, and broadens its meaning, giving the positive implications of the command.[15] However, this is not some new thing that Jesus makes up. Jesus is showing his followers God's heart behind the command. Jesus' Sermon on the Mount, is in large part an exposition of Deuteronomy!

Jesus also quotes Deuteronomy as the single most important teaching in the Old Testament. In Matthew 22, we read that a group of Pharisees get together in order to test Jesus. They send an expert, a teacher of the law, to test Jesus with a question. He says, "Teacher, what is the greatest commandment in the law?" This is a difficult question. Jewish rabbis had counted 613 separate commands in the Old Testament. So, this expert is asking Jesus to pick which single command is the most important out of over 600 options. In reply, Jesus quotes the *Shema* from Deuteronomy 6. Jesus says, "'Love the LORD your God with all your heart and with all your soul and with all your mind.' This is the first and greatest commandment." When asked to pick the most important commandment from the entire Old Testament, Jesus quotes the central verse of Deuteronomy.

15. For this understanding of Jesus' teaching in the Sermon on the Mount, I am indebted to the work of John Burgess, particularly *After Baptism*. See also Hopkins, "Understanding," 41–58, esp. 48–55: the negative minimums imply positive maximums. This is clear when Deuteronomy expounds the Ten Words with positive obligations.

When asked what God requires of his people, Jesus again quotes Deuteronomy. In Luke 18:18, a rich young ruler comes to Jesus and says, "Good teacher, what must I do to inherit eternal life?" In other words, what does God require of me? What does God want from me? It is worth noting that there are many things that Jesus could have said. He could have given a sermon. He could have quoted Micah 6:8, "He has shown you, O mortal, what is good. And what does the LORD require of you? To act justly and to love mercy and to walk humbly with your God." However, Jesus does not say any of these things. Jesus goes to Deuteronomy. Jesus responds in Luke 18:20, "You know the commandments: 'You shall not commit adultery, you shall not murder, you shall not steal, you shall not give false testimony, honor your father and mother.'" When asked what God requires of his people, Jesus quotes Deuteronomy.

Our last example is that when Jesus teaches his disciples what to do with someone who has hurt them or sinned against them, he again turns to Deuteronomy for instruction. In Matthew, Jesus instructs his disciples, "If your brother or sister sins, go and point out their fault, just between the two of you. If they listen to you, you have won them over. But if they will not listen, take one or two others along, so that 'every matter may be established by the testimony of two or three witnesses.'" Establishing things by two or three witnesses is drawn from Deut 19:15.

New Testament Writers Apply Deuteronomy to Jesus

The five examples above demonstrate that Jesus considered Deuteronomy to be God's discipleship manual. In addition to Jesus himself, many of the New Testament authors also called heavily upon Deuteronomy. When they were seeking to explain the meaning of the life, death and resurrection of Jesus, they quoted Deuteronomy often.[16] They quoted passages from Deuteronomy and applied them to the life, ministry, death and resurrection of Jesus. We see several examples of that in the following chart.[17] The items in the chart have been grouped topically according to the claim that the New Testament authors are making about Jesus by quoting Deuteronomy. This list is not meant to be exhaustive.

16. Block. *Deuteronomy*, 26–27.

17. Lundbom, *Deuteronomy*, 950–955.

Assertion	Passage cited from Deuteronomy	New Testament Passage
Jesus fulfills the law	Deuteronomy 5:17–21: "You shall not murder. You shall not commit adultery. You shall not steal . . . You shall not covet your neighbor's wife."	Romans 13:8–10: "The commandments, You shall not commit adultery, You shall not murder, You shall not steal, You shall not covet . . . are summed up in this one command: 'Love your neighbor as yourself.'" (Completely fulfilled in Jesus)
No favoritism in salvation	Deuteronomy 10:17: "For the LORD your God is God of gods and LORD of lords . . .who shows no partiality."	Acts 10:34: "Peter began to speak: "I now realize how true it is that God does not show favoritism."
Jesus is Lord	Deuteronomy 10:17: "For the LORD your God is God of gods and LORD of lords, the great God."	Revelation 17:14: "the Lamb will triumph over them because he is LORD of lords and King of kings." (also cited in Revelation 19:16)
Christ paid our penalty on the cross	Deuteronomy 21:23: "Anyone who is hung on a pole is under God's curse."	Galatians 3:13: "Christ redeemed us from the curse of the law . . . "Cursed is everyone who is hung on a pole." (I Peter 2:24, Acts 5:30; 10:39)
We live by faith in Christ, not by works of the law	Deuteronomy 27:26: "Cursed is anyone who does not uphold the words of this law by carrying them out."	Galatians 3:10: "as it is written: "Cursed is everyone who does not continue to do everything written in the Book of the Law."
Trust Christ for salvation	Deuteronomy 30:14: "The word is very near you; it is in your mouth and in your heart so you may obey it."	Romans 10:8, 9: "What does it say? 'The word is near you; it is in your mouth and in your heart,' that is, the message concerning faith that we proclaim."
Christ is coming again	Deuteronomy 11:13, 14: "So if you faithfully obey the commands I am giving you today . . . then I will send rain on your land in its season, both autumn and spring rains."	James 5:7, 8: "Be patient, then, brothers and sisters, until the Lord's coming. See how the farmer waits . . . patiently . . . for the autumn and spring rains. You too, be patient and stand firm, because the Lord's coming is near."

MEDITATING ON THE TORAH DAY AND NIGHT

As a help for meditating on the Torah day and night, below are some of the key verses from Deuteronomy: 5:1–22; 6:1–9; 6:20–25; 8:1–3; 30:19–20.

Chapter 10

The Message of the Torah

In the *Star Wars* saga, the ever-looming goal was the ultimate defeat of the evil Empire. Each episode saw a partial victory, a step in the right direction, but final resolution required a series of installments, each making its own contribution. In the end, the objective was achieved. Once that occurred, the necessity of each episode to the final victory is appreciated.

The Torah is like this. Each part of the Torah is a necessary part of the whole. Each Torah part has now been studied, and from its content, structure, and themes a message has been discerned. The message of the Torah arises from what we have discovered in the parts and the sequence in which these elements are presented. The message of each Torah book will be repeated here, and then a comprehensive theme will be distilled from them. The chapter will conclude by bringing this message to life as the Torah does, painting it in the colors and hues of two fascinating characters named Abraham and Moses.

THE MESSAGE OF THE TORAH BOOKS

The message of Genesis: God created the world as a temple-house where he could live in intimate friendship with the people he created. They would serve him in his temple as human agents of his reign, worshipping him, extending his kingdom, and finding abundant life in him. But sin entered God's house and brought death: alienation from God, from other people, and from God's good gifts. God responded by making a grand promise to defeat evil, to which he called people to respond with faith and obedience so that they could be renewed in life, and he made covenants with those who believed,[1] *promising friendship with him and blessing. He also called believers to a mission to share their great God and his promise with the nations.*

The message of Exodus: The presence of God is the richest treasure we can know; so God reveals his character to us in the story of how he liberates people from bondage and then invites us to believe him and enter into a committed relationship with him akin to marriage; saying "I do!" joins us forever to his presence, providing freedom from slavery to our sins, and wisdom for abundant life with him.

The message of Leviticus: God wants to dwell with his people in love and intimacy but because he is holy and his bride is not, he establishes both procedures for approaching him appropriately and mediators to stand between himself and his people. These allow atonement to be made for sin so that God and his people can live together in harmony and joy. He then provides procedures for his people to maintain holiness to enable them to live happily ever after with him, and to love their neighbor as themselves (Lev 19:18).

The message of Numbers: Believers who have seen the power and grace of God have every reason to trust and obey him. But over the long haul, as fear and temptations arise, those who were faithful may choose to forget God's goodness and choose poorly. They may opt to believe what circumstances suggest or complain because they cannot understand what God is doing. They may prefer present comfort to future blessing. Or they may choose to trust God's promises and act in faith, fixing their hope on what God has promised them. One path leads to loss of blessing, conflict and ultimately death; the other leads to blessing, resolution of conflicts, hope, and ultimately life.

The message of Deuteronomy: Because God loves us and desires for us to love him God offers us a real choice between life and death. This is a choice that each one of us will have to make. Deuteronomy is comprised of three sermons in which Moses encourages us to choose life through faith in God. We grow in faith and obedience by meditating on the Torah day and night. One way that this faith and obedience to God's instructions shows itself in our lives is caring for the poor and the vulnerable.

1. Actually, some covenants, like the one with Noah, are not dependent upon faith.

THE MESSAGE OF THE TORAH

The Theme of the Torah

Students of Scripture have long wrestled with the theme of the Torah, i.e., the main topic that drives the plot. The diversity of conclusions might suggest that the Torah is as clear as a glass of chocolate milk! But plots are like that. The pieces fall into place slowly and all is not clear until the end. Early in *Star Wars* it was not clear who Palpatine was, but it eventually became so. Likewise, the theme of the Torah has been hard to discern because scholars often examined the parts (Genesis, etc.) rather than the whole. In recent times, there has been more attention to the whole Torah.

As a result, it appears that a consensus has been developing.[2] In the twentieth century, Martin Noth (1902–68) discerned five themes in the Torah.[3] They are Guidance out of Egypt, Guidance into an Arable Land, Promise to the Patriarchs, Guidance in the Wilderness, and Revelation at Sinai.[4] While not coherently related, Noth's themes are accurate.

The other important twentieth-century voice was the gifted scholar Gerhard von Rad (1901–71).[5] He saw the theme of the Pentateuch as chronicling the progressive fulfillment of the three promises God made to Abraham: *descendants* in a *land* with a special *relationship* with God. He believed that the promise of descendants was fulfilled by Exodus, and that the promise of a special relationship was accomplished when Israel became God's people at Sinai. But regarding the land promise, "throughout the five books there is a looking forward to the unrealized hope of settlement, something which was not achieved until the time of Joshua."[6] Von Rad presents a more cohesive approach to the Torah.

2. My treatment here depends upon Wenham, *Pentateuch*, 145–47.

3. Noth assumed the documentary hypothesis and held that the stages of the Torah's growth held the key to its meaning. But "Noth offers no hard evidence for his theory" (Wenham, *Pentateuch*, 147). Clines, *Pentateuch*, 9, writes, "the sources and pre-history of our present texts are for the most part entirely hypothetical," and of the conclusions he states, "It's firm results turn out to be meager." Wenham, *Pentateuch*, 150, calls this approach "speculative. We really do not know how biblical books came to be written, especially in their early stages, so to base our interpretation of them on guesses about how and when they came into existence is a very dubious procedure."

4. Clines, *Pentateuch*, 17.

5. I depend here upon Wenham, *Pentateuch*, 147–49. Von Rad also assumed the documentary hypothesis.

6. Wenham, *Pentateuch*, 149.

A major step forward occurred in 1978 when David Clines published *The Theme of the Pentateuch*.[7] He emphasized that repeated reading of the text of the Torah as a unified whole was more useful than theories about it's development, as Noth and von Rad had assumed.[8] He also concluded the key was the three-part promise to Abraham: *descendants* in a *relationship* with God in a *land*. But he added that each book in the Pentateuch is future oriented.[9] "The theme of the Pentateuch is the partial fulfillment—which implies also the partial non-fulfillment—of the promise to or blessing of the patriarchs."[10]

Wenham considers Clines's view a great advance. Among other things, "Clines makes an important contribution by [pointing out that] God promises to the patriarchs what was given to the human race at creation but lost through the fall: land, descendants and a close relationship with God."[11] However, he adds that blessing is an important missing element of the promise to Abraham. Wenham improves our understanding by setting the themes in the larger context of the Torah story. "The theme of the Pentateuch is the fulfillment of the promises to the patriarchs, which are a reaffirmation of God's original intentions for the human race, through God's mercy and the collaboration of Moses. . . . [But] complete fulfillment awaits the future."[12]

We have shown that a broad consensus about the Torah's theme has been developing. The chocolate milk has become a clear pool. Based upon this book's conclusions, and noting that the promise theme begins before Abraham,[13] the following Torah theme statement is offered. *The theme of the Torah is the fulfillment of God's promise in Genesis 3:15 to restore Eden's intimate relationship between the king and his people so that humans can serve God and experience abundant life now while they wait for the complete fulfillment of his promise in eternity.* This statement is quite like that of Walter Kaiser.[14]

The Message of the Torah: Choose Life

The message of the Torah refers to *how* the theme works out, to what the author wants the audience to believe and do. The message is derived from combining the component parts.

7. See Wenham, *Pentateuch*, 150–53.
8. Clines, *Pentateuch*, 5–9.
9. Clines, *Pentateuch*, 25–27.
10. Clines, *Pentateuch*, 29. He elaborates, but this is the core of his statement.
11. Wenham, *Pentateuch*, 153.
12. Wenham, *Pentateuch*, 157.
13. Kaiser, *Promise-Plan*, 34–67.
14. Kaiser, *Promise-Plan*, 34–67.

The full Torah message can be stated as follows. *To fulfill his promise to restore the edenic relationship, so that people can return to serving the king and enjoy abundant life, in Genesis and Exodus God calls a people into a covenant relationship to know him (Gen 4–50, Exod 1–18) and to spread (Exod 19:6) the blessing of the knowledge of his reign (Exod 19–40) to all the lands of the earth* (Genesis 12:1–3). *In Leviticus we learn that maintaining an intimate relationship between God and his people requires sacrifice to atone for sin, which is practiced by faith and results in a holy life toward God and entails loving one's neighbor as oneself (Lev 19:18).In Numbers we learn that maintaining that relationship requires that God's people trust God daily and choose to remain faithful to him over the long haul. So, in Deuteronomy we see that people must choose life over death, life which comes by loving, trusting, and obeying the king. But inheriting God's promise, which sustains his people on their arduous journey, comes in two stages: God grants his sustaining presence now but calls his people to live in hope (faith directed toward the future), waiting for the complete fulfillment of the promise, when they are ushered into his eternal kingdom.*

The full restoration of Eden is in eternity, as the Torah's waiting theme instructs us. C. S. Lewis said that the believer's life on earth is the title page of the book that is their life, and that eternity writes the book itself with each successive chapter being better than the last one! This is the grand hope that awaits those who believe in Christ![15]

The Torah summarizes its message at the end in Deuteronomy 30:19–20: "I have set before you life and death, blessing and curse. Therefore, choose life, that you and your offspring may live, loving the LORD your God, obeying his voice and holding fast to him, for he is your life and length of days."

The Argument Illustrated: Abraham and Moses

We have examined the ideas and themes that run through the Torah. The Torah itself also embeds these lessons in the stories of the two main characters: Abraham and Moses. It *shows* as much as it tells. Here we maintain that the Torah presents them as a contrast, portraying Abraham as *the* champion of the Torah.

The Torah depicts Abraham as the book's hero in a series of ways: (1) Abraham is held up as the paradigm for the nation; (2) it paints Abraham as particularly close to God; (3) it shows that Abraham's obedience to God outshone Moses' obedience; (4) it records epitaphs over their lives that make Moses pale in the brilliant light of Abraham's obedience; thereby (5) it

15. Lewis, *The Last Battle*, vol. 7 of The Chronicles of Narnia (New York: Macmillan, 1956).

points out that Abraham outshone Moses in faith. Paul seems to have read the Torah this way, five times naming Abraham, not Moses, the "father" of all who believe in Romans 4:11–17.

It is important to see that this does not mean Abraham was perfect; far from it! The first episode in Abraham's story after he obeys God's call to go to Canaan is a serious failure of faith (Gen 12:10–20), and other sins and failures follow. We are not saying Abraham was a flawless model. But he is still the Torah's poster boy for how to live well.

Abraham is the Paradigm for Israel

The first indication that Abraham is our model comes from the Torah's structure.[16] Sailhamer writes that "the events of the Pentateuch are divided between those before and those during the giving of the Law."[17] While the bulk of the Torah is devoted Moses and the law,[18] the primary character in Genesis is Abraham. That defines Genesis as "what came before the law." So, the Torah contrasts Abraham, the hero before the Law, with Moses, the man of Law.

Further, Genesis portrays Abraham as the paradigm for the nation in several ways. His faith is held up (Gen 15:6) as the first stated example of faith bringing righteousness. Genesis also presents his life as foreshadowing the nation's history in a series of ways. Abraham goes to Egypt where God "plagues" Pharaoh, and then releases Abraham to return to Canaan (Gen 12:10–20). This parallels what God did for Moses' generation. God's testing of Israel in Exodus 15 echoes God's testing of Abraham (Gen 22:1). Abraham's waiting for God's promised son and land are examples to Israel that God calls his people to wait, and that he fulfills his promises. Abraham's blessing of the nations (e.g., Gen 14:11–24; 20:17) represents Israel's calling. In these ways Abraham, the father of the nation, is also the exemplar of what the nation is to be.

Abraham Walked with God

Another way that the Torah trumpets Abraham's top-dog status is by portraying him as particularly close to God. Special intimacy with God is

16. Westermann, *Genesis*, 2:28, asserted, "no single figure of the Old Testament could have such an all-embracing significance as Abraham."

17. Sailhamer, *Pentateuch*, 71.

18. That is, Exodus, Leviticus, and Numbers 1–14. Numbers 15–36 covers the forty years of wilderness wandering, then Deuteronomy records the last three or so days of Moses' life.

portrayed early in the Torah by saying that someone walked with God.[19] The first instance is in Genesis 3:8. Immediately after Adam and Eve ate the forbidden fruit, we read, "And they heard the sound of the LORD God *walking* in the garden in the cool of the day." Though the close relationship with God has been ruptured, their closeness to God in their edenic state is portrayed as God coming to "walk" with them. Hereafter, this becomes the image of special closeness to God. Next, "Enoch walked with God" (Gen 5:22), so "he was not, for God took him" (Gen 5:24). Enoch's closeness to God meant being spared death! "Noah walked with God" (Genesis 6:9) and he and his family were spared through the flood. Only two other people in the Torah are ever described this way: Abraham (Gen 17:1; 24:40; 48:15) and Isaac (Gen 48:15). Though Moses is uniquely honored (Numbers 12:3), no one after Abraham and Isaac walked with God.

Abraham Outshone Moses in Obedience

The Torah shows that Abraham outshone Moses by the way their stories are structured. Abraham's life is framed with two grand acts of obedience, reflecting his powerful faith. The first is his call-story (Genesis 12:1–4). God commands Abraham[20] to leave all he knows and travel to a distant land, and Abraham obeys without hesitation: "So Abram went" (Gen 12:4). The Torah also ends Abraham's story with an even greater act of faith which echoes his call story. God tests Abraham by telling him "to go to the land of Moriah" and offer Isaac as a sacrifice (Gen 22:1–2). Abraham's response mirrors his call story: "So Abraham rose early in the morning" and went (22:3). This call was more demanding than the first. Since Isaac's death would have destroyed God's promise of a "great nation," obedience seemed to threaten everything. Yet Abraham obeyed without hesitation! He is a good role model.

The Torah handles Moses biography very differently. It frames Moses' life story with two grand examples of disobedience, acts that reflect failures of faith. Whereas Abraham's response to God's call is brief and beautiful, Moses' response to God's call is long and ugly. After God speaks from the burning bush, two chapters record Moses' objections and excuses.

Exodus 3:11: But Moses said to God, "Who am I that I should go to Pharaoh and bring the children of Israel out of Egypt?" (God then responds to Moses' words in 3:12–22.)

19. Wenham, *Genesis 1–15*, 127.

20. His name is changed from Abram to Abraham later, but we will call him Abraham throughout.

Exodus 4:1: "Then Moses answered, "But behold, they will not believe me or listen to my voice, for they will say, 'The LORD did not appear to you.'" (God answers in 4:2–9.)

Exodus 4:10: "But Moses said to the LORD, 'Oh, my LORD, I am not eloquent, either in the past or since you have spoken to your servant, but I am slow of speech and of tongue.'" (God tries to reassure Moses in 4:11–12.)

Exodus 4:13: "But [Moses] said, 'Oh, my LORD, please send someone else.'" (At this point "the anger of the LORD was kindled against Moses," 4:14–17.)

Moses' second response is as subtle as brass knuckles (4:1). God urged Moses to accept his call by saying that Israel "will listen to your voice" (3:18). Moses throws these words back in God's face, retorting (literally in the Hebrew), "But, behold, *not* 'they will believe me or *listen to my voice*'" (4:1). He directly contradicts God by quoting God's exact words and denying them! In this, he mimics the serpent who contradicted God directly saying, "*Not* 'you will surely die'" (Gen 3:4; 2:17). Notice that God's answers to Moses become shorter and shorter until God finally loses his temper. Moses obeys—after God reasons, cajoles and finally erupts! Such is Moses' initial encounter with God!

Moses' self-described end is tragic. The climactic episode that seals his fate is recoded in Numbers 20.[21] For a second time Israel has no water in the wilderness and this time God tells Moses not to "strike" (Exod 17:6), but to "speak" to the rock (Num 20:8). But Moses lost his temper (20:9–10) and disobeyed God, striking the rock in full view of all Israel. This flagrant, public disobedience was a major failing and God decrees the devastating result: "Because you did not believe in me, to uphold me as holy in the eyes of the people of Israel, therefore you shall not bring this assembly into the land that I have given them." Moses would die alone, excluded from what he sought throughout his long years of leadership of Israel. Though honored (Deut 34:1–8), he died in discipline, and excluded from God's promise. The Torah thus begins with Adam and Eve failing in obedience and excluded from Eden and it ends with Moses' parallel experience, failing in obedience and excluded from the Promised land.

By writing their biographies as opposites Moses repented in print, acknowledging that Abraham was the star whom Moses could not equal. While both men had strengths and weaknesses, Moses' contrasting portraits teach that Abraham began well and ended better, whereas Moses began poorly and ended badly.

21. Numbers 20 is not literally the end of Moses' life, but it is effectively the end, with the rest of Numbers (22–36) preparing Israel to enter Canaan after Moses' death, and Deuteronomy recording the last few days of Moses' life.

Abraham's Epitaph Outshines Moses' Epitaph

Another way the Torah exalts Abraham over Moses is in the epitaphs that God gave to each man. Abraham's epitaph is recorded shortly after his death. God declares, "Abraham obeyed my voice and kept my charge, my commandments, my statutes and my laws" (Gen 26:5). Two things are striking. First, the man known for his faith (Gen 15:6) is credited with obedience. This *states* what was *shown* by framing his life with examples of faith: faith produces obedience. The other striking thing is the surprising *way* his obedience is described! To say that Abraham "kept my charge, my commandments, my statutes and my laws" is a normal way to describe obedience to the *Mosaic Law* (e.g., Deut 6:1).[22] God's epitaph is that Abraham obeyed the Mosaic Law (or its spirit) *before it was ever given*![23]

Moses' epitaph, recorded in Numbers 20:12, is noticeably different![24] While Moses disobeys, God's evaluation unearths the root problem: "The LORD said to Moses and Aaron, 'Because you *did not believe in me*, to uphold me as holy in the eyes of the people of Israel, therefore you shall not bring this assembly into the land.'" Treating God this way is as safe as picnicking on the train tracks. The startling truth is that Moses' failure to "uphold me as *holy* in *the eyes of the people*" parallels the earlier sin of Nadab and Abihu. There God explains why he put them to death: "Among those who are near me I will be *sanctified*, and *before all the people* I will be glorified.'" (Lev 10:3; the same Hebrew word is used for "holy" and "sanctified"). God's epitaph over Moses, the man of law, is that he failed due to weak faith, while God's epitaph over Abraham, the man of faith, is that he obeyed the law! Abraham's obedience, without knowing the Law, was better than that of Moses, who gave the law! Because Moses' root was weak the fruit was also.

Abraham Outshone Moses in Faith

We have already suggested that the reason Abraham outshone Moses in obedience is that he outshone him in faith. The Torah teaches that obedience springs from faith and disobedience reveals weak (or no) faith. If disobedience is rooted in poor faith, as Numbers 20:10–12 shows, obedience is rooted in strong faith.

22. Wenham, *Genesis 16–50*, 190.

23. Sailhamer, *Pentateuch*, 66–71; Westermann, *Genesis 12–36*, 424–25; Waltke, *Genesis*, 368.

24. See Sailhamer, *Pentateuch*, 72–78.

The author of Hebrews perceived it this way. In Hebrews 11, the famous "hall of faith" passage, Abraham is mentioned but twice. First, "By faith Abraham obeyed when he was called to go out to a place that he was to receive as an inheritance. . . . By faith he went to live in the land of promise" (Heb 11:8–9). Second is Heb 11:18: "By faith Abraham, when he was tested, offered up Isaac." Hebrews cites the two examples of faith that frame Abraham's life story!

Note further that while Moses is a major figure cited for his faith (11:24–28), "the writer devotes more space to Abraham as an exemplar of faith than to any other OT figure (vv 8–12, 17–19),"[25] a total of twelve verses compared to Moses' six.[26] Earlier in his book when calling his readers to faith in 6:9–12, the one exemplar of faith he cites is Abraham (6:13).[27]

Hebrews shows that faith is the root of obedience by repeating the refrain, "By faith X [obeyed/acted]." "By faith Abel offered" (11:4); "By faith Noah . . . constructed" (11:7), etc. The author is *showing* the person's faith *by what they did*, explaining faith as the motivation for the actions. Where did the author of Hebrews get this idea? The answer is from the Torah! It is widely acknowledged that *showing* rather than *telling* the reader is the norm in biblical stories.[28] For example, the author of Samuel does not say, "Lo, David did evil in the sight of the Lord by disobeying the Torah command that a king not collect a harem" (Deut 17:17). Instead, he *shows* the reader this by reporting each time David married another woman (1 Sam 18:27; 25:39–44; 2 Sam 3:2–5; 12:24). He expects the reader to note David's persistent disobedience,[29] i.e., to discern a person's character by their actions.

This is how the Hebrews explains faith. "Faith is the assurance of things hoped for, the conviction of things not seen" (Heb 11:1). He defines faith as being so assured that God's promises *will* take place that people act.[30] Hebrews 11 is a history of faith shown by actions.

We conclude that Moses shows the reader that Abraham is "*the* biblical hero of faith."[31] He does so by showing that Abraham walked with God better than Moses, that his obedience outshone Moses' obedience, and

25. Lane, *Hebrews 9–13*, loc. 7789 of 22827, Kindle.

26. Waltke, *Genesis*, 194.

27. Lane, *Hebrews 9–13*, loc. 6589 of 22827, Kindle.

28. Indirect characterization, by showing, rather than direct characterization, by stating what a character is like, is the norm: Bar-Efrat, *Narrative Art*.

29. Note that this pattern also shows the reader that David's sin with Bathsheba is not to be read as a brief moment of indiscretion, but as the escalation of David's long habit of sexual disobedience.

30. Bruce, *Hebrews*, 277–81.

31. Waltke, *Genesis*, 194.

that Abraham's epitaph outshone Moses epitaph, *because* Abraham's faith outshone Moses' faith. Abraham *shows* that the root of faith yields the fruit of obedience. Perfect Abraham absolutely was not; faith-model Abraham assuredly was; standard Abraham definitely does set! From Abraham decidedly we glean, "Mind what you have learned; save you it can."

Conclusion: The Argument of the Torah Revisited

We have seen that the Torah summarizes its argument as, "choose life" (Deut 30:19–20). Since it illustrates this lesson in a contrast between Abraham and Moses, the Torah message may be stated in a short form as, *Choose life by living by faith like Abraham!*[32]

If this is correct, we would expect Abraham's life to portray all the major Torah lessons we have gleaned from the Torah books, and this turns out to be the case. He is *the* biblical example of faith and of obedience and models a covenant relationship with God. He is the fountainhead of the people God created to bless the world with abundant life by knowing God. He is a model of being blessed and of sharing blessing with the nations. He practiced sacrifice before the Law mandated it and experienced the holiness that sacrifice brings.[33] His faith grew over time. Over the long haul, and when the most grievous test came (Gen 22), he chose to remain faithful and obedient, even when he could not understand (Heb 11:19). When he offered his son to God, Abraham was really offering himself to God. In offering the son who he "loved" (Gen 22:2), the Torah shows that Abraham loved God even more. That is why Abraham was willing to do for nothing what others would not do for anything. He exemplifies loving neighbor as oneself (Gen 13, 14). Finally, because he believed God, he is an example of patient waiting for God's promises, especially the promised land. To meditate on the life of Abraham is to observe the lessons of the Torah in action!

Thus, the Torah states its core message at the beginning and at the end, as Morales observes: "within the garden YHWH set both a tree of life and a tree of the knowledge of good and evil. Taken together, with their fruits procuring life and death respectively, the trees may be seen to function like the Torah, imploring Adam to choose life."[34] Choose life by living by faith like Abraham!

32. In this I resemble Sailhamer, *Pentateuch*.

33. Further, while the Hebrew root for "holy" occurs only once in Genesis (2:3), Noah is said to be "blameless" (Gen 6:9), an term very similar to "holy," and Abraham is commanded to be "blameless" (Gen 17:1). The same term is used of God in Deut 32:4 ("perfect") where it parallels "without iniquity, just and upright," i.e., holy.

34. Morales, *Leviticus*, 54.

THE TORAH, THE MOSAIC LAW, AND THE CHRISTIAN

Our final task is to clarify the relation of the Torah, the Mosaic Law, and the Christian.[35] We saw earlier that while most think of the Torah as equivalent to "the Law of Moses," this is inadequate since over 40 percent of the Torah is not laws. We saw that the Torah is better viewed as a biography of Moses, but that this also fails to do justice to the material. Twenty percent of the Torah is biography of Moses (if the laws are excluded), another 20 percent of it consists of biographies of Abraham, Jacob and Joseph in Genesis, and there is a good amount of other history and poetry as well.[36] Since equal portions of the Torah before and after the law are devoted to biographies, a better characterization would be that the Torah consists of biographies of those before the law, preeminently Abraham, and after the Law, i.e., Moses. The Torah contains the Mosaic Covenant but is not identical with it.

Sailhamer extends these insights to defend the following propositions. Since the Torah is best characterized as biography, its purpose is to contrast life before the law with life under the law by profiling the two main characters who exemplify each, Abraham and Moses.[37] The purpose of the laws in the Torah is not to teach the Mosaic laws to believers of all time, or even primarily to ancient Israel, though it was Israel's law. Instead, the laws in the Torah are selective, just enough of the entire Mosaic code "to give the reader an understanding of the nature of the Mosaic Law and God's purpose in giving it to Israel. . . . The laws in the Pentateuch are not there to tell the *reader* how to live but rather to tell the reader how Moses was to live under the law."[38] Their primary purpose was "to answer the question of how well Moses carried out his calling."[39]

What is the verdict on Moses? Clearly, with all his gifts and praiseworthy qualities, Moses failed. He could not live under the law, and like the generation he led out of Egypt, he died in the wilderness. From this Sailhamer concludes that the Torah is an argument *about* the failure of law as a good system of life, and that the faith of Abraham is a better model than the law of Moses. The Mosaic law was to be obeyed by Israel: it was *their law*. But the primary purpose of incorporating the law into the Torah was to show that Abraham was a better model for believers *before* the law than was Moses who lived by the law. Israel's failure to keep it, which eventually led

35. I am indebted in what follows to Sailhamer, both *Meaning* and *Theology*.

36. Sailhamer, *Theology*, 259.

37. Sailhamer, *Theology*, 255.

38. Sailhamer, *Theology*, 256.

39. Sailhamer, *Theology*, 255–56.

to their exile from the land, parallels Moses' failure and exclusion from the land, both of which echo the biography of Adam and Eve. Thus, the Torah begins with failure to keep God's command in the Garden and it ends with failure to keep God's law outside the land.

All of this sounds suspiciously like the Apostle Paul because the Torah taught it to Paul! Paul declared (Gal 3:23–25), "Now before faith came, we were held captive under the law, imprisoned until the coming faith would be revealed. So then, the law was our guardian until Christ came, in order that we might be justified by faith. But now that faith has come, we are no longer under a guardian."

The Torah is an argument about how to get blessing. The answer is by the obedience that comes from faith like Abraham's, which yields better obedience that life by law.

So how does all of this relate to Christians? First, since the Torah is not identical with the Mosaic Law, Christians can be free from the Mosaic Law (Romans 6:14; Heb 8:13) and still see the Torah as authoritative Scripture in the fullest sense. In part this is because the Torah is teaching that faith is the path to blessing. This is the lesson of the New Covenant and the New Testament. An analogy may help. Jesus walked on water. No Christian reads this as a lesson about what they should do. Instead it is read as uniquely true of Jesus but holding lessons for Christians. Just so, the primary way to profit from the Mosai Law is not to use it as a manual of rules, but to learn about faith and God's character through it.

Those Mosaic laws that articulate eternal truths are restated in the New Testament and Christians are bound by them. But the primary function of the Torah laws is to school us in the failure of human works and the necessity of living by faith. The Torah's message is that living by law weakens faith while living by faith strengthens obedience. As Calvin expressed it, people are justified by faith alone, but not by a faith that remains alone.

Chapter 11

A Guide to Reading, Teaching, and Preaching the Torah

THE TORAH IS GOD'S DISCIPLESHIP MANUAL

If someone wished to become a Jedi apprentice, they were supposed to be approved by the Jedi council and then begin training with a Jedi Master, as Anakin Skywalker wished to do with Qui-Gon Jinn. That was the established path. Is there an established path for Christian discipleship?

Sometimes it seems that Christians have a hundred different ideas about the right path to spiritual maturity! *This* book, *that* prayer seminar, *this* experience, *that* neglected doctrine ("self-esteem" was the "new Reformation" for a while). I once read a book by a devout Christian carpet layer who believed he had found *the secret* that accounted for our spiritual impotence. He had learned that Paul's words, "We who are alive and remain to the coming of the Lord" (1 Thess. 4:15), show Paul expected to live until Jesus came. He then explained his great insight: that *clearly meant* that any believer with strong faith would never die physically (really!). If you wanted to die, he said, go ahead; but he himself was going to live until Jesus came, if that was 500 years from now! (Sad that Paul was so weak!)

Most Christians have been more realistic! J. I. Packer pointed out that Christians have a long tradition of discipling new believers by a three-part approach.[1] New Christians were taught how Christians *behave* through the Ten Commandments. They learned how to *pray* using the Lord's Prayer as a model. Finally, instruction in Christian *doctrine* was from the Apostles Creed. Two of these three are directly biblical, while the third is an early (eighth century AD in its final form) summary of Christian belief accepted by Roman Catholic, Eastern Orthodox, and Protestant Christians. Laudable, wholesome and beneficial as this traditional practice is (really!), I propose that God intended the Torah to serve as *the* biblical training manual for believers![2] The Torah spells out *the* path to discipleship, the God-established road to spiritual growth, by teaching all of the core lessons that believers of all ages need. Further, it does so *not* primarily by announcing abstract principles, but by embedding the lessons in the lives of frail and struggling people like us. In addition, it does so in a *sequence* that establishes how the elements fit together. Whether one is a new believer or a veteran Christian, the Torah is *the* foundational study! This chapter is to help you grow through the Torah or to help others do so.

HOW THE TORAH INSTRUCTS BELIEVERS

We have already discussed how the Torah instructs God's people of all ages. But additional discussion is appropriate about this. Leder's model is helpful on this critical issue. While I draw from him, the material will be developed somewhat differently here, consistent with what has been argued from the Torah about its message.[3]

Leder is astute when he argues that the desert narrative provides enduring instruction for "God's people of every generation."[4] Leder sees the exodus from Egypt as teaching believers of all ages that God's redemption entails a separation from their past life, as Israel was separated by God from its slavery in Egypt.[5] As Israel was redeemed from building Pharaoh's cities as slaves (Exod 1:11) to voluntarily building a house for God (Exod 25–40), so God's people have been redeemed from their past sins to labor for God's kingdom.

1. Packer, *Christian*.

2. Milgrom recognizes something very like this regarding Leviticus when he comments "Leviticus, so long thought to be esoteric and irrelevant, will turn out to be an old-new guide toward achieving quality life." See his *Leviticus*, 2004, xiii.

3. Leder, *Waiting*, esp. 195–203. I am indebted to Leder's discussion in this section.

4. Leder, *Waiting*, 196. Leder sees the Torah as a catechism, or instruction manual, but my use of this term predates reading his discussion.

5. Leder, *Waiting*, 197–99.

Exodus also teaches that God tests his people (Exod 15:25) to teach them obedience (Exod 16:4), as he tested Abraham (Gen 22:1; see James 1:12). The many trying circumstances God led Israel to face in the wilderness are examples for us. The wilderness is also symbolic of the life of the believer in a hostile world where danger and enemies surround us. But now as then, God's presence is our strength. In our wilderness journey we too experience "God's surprising provision of daily sustenance."[6]

Leviticus instructs us that holiness is serious business by detailing how God can be approached by unholy people like us. The "fear of the Lord" is a critical theme throughout the Torah.[7] When we read in Exodus that Israel feared Pharaoh (Exod 14:10–13), but learned to fear the Lord (Exod 14:31) after seeing God's plagues, we are instructed regarding what is proper to fear. As Leder puts it, referring to the pillar of fire that symbolized God's presence in the wilderness, Israel's wilderness journey "teaches all generations of God's desert people how to live with that fire in their midst."[8]

Leder also proposes that, like Israel, believers are God's army (Numbers 1:3). This reminds us that conflict is the normal experience of the believer. God is "a man of war" (Exod 15:3) because God and his people will always have enemies, as Pharaoh opposed Israel. So God is able to fight for us and with us.[9] This is why Numbers 10:35 declares, "And whenever the ark set out, Moses said, 'Arise, O LORD, and let your enemies be scattered, and let those who hate you flee before you.'"

Numbers teaches God's people of all generations that in our struggles, we must choose to be faithful to God. When our resources do not seem adequate (Exodus 15:22–26; Numbers 11:1–3), or when God's leaders do not please us (Numbers 16), or when we are afraid of doing what God commands (Numbers 14), or misunderstandings arise among God's people (Numbers 32–33), will we trust him and obey? The wilderness wanderings also teach us "the limitations of human wisdom."[10] Israel often could not see what God was doing or feared what he allowed, and so trusted their own wisdom as Eve had done in the Garden. It always turned out badly! Their failings in faith instruct us.

Jesus was also called into the wilderness (Mark 1:1–13). Mark presents Jesus' entire life as a wilderness experience, as ours is in this world. In that setting, and throughout his life, Jesus was tempted in the ways we are, and

6. Leder, *Waiting*, 199.
7. Leder, *Waiting*, 208–9.
8. Leder, *Waiting*, 209.
9. Leder, *Waiting*, 201–2.
10. Leder, *Waiting*, 209.

yet he did not sin (Heb 4:15). He "was successful where Israel (Matt 4:1–17) and Adam (Luke 4:1–13) had failed."[11] He is a better model for us than Israel often was.

The Torah makes waiting for the land a major theme. But Wenham makes a remarkable observation when he states, "the promise that the land would be Israel's 'everlasting possession' means that even when they are living in the land its fulfillment is incomplete."[12] They possess it, but not the fullness of its possession! This is a picture of the condition of Israel when she inherited the land under Joshua, and of the believer now. We now possess the new covenant blessings, but the fullness of those blessings is yet to come for us. This is the "already" and the "not yet" of the Christian life. The land we await is an eternal city (Heb 11:10). Christians, like ancient Israel, still live in Deuteronomy 8:2–3: "And you shall remember the whole way that the LORD your God has led you . . . in the wilderness, that he might humble you, testing you to know what was in your heart, whether you would keep his commandments or not. And he humbled you and let you hunger and fed you . . . that he might make you know that man does not live by bread alone, but man lives by every word that comes from the mouth of the LORD." So, believers now live graced with the continual presence of our God with us, our great treasure, but we also live in hope, waiting for our savior to fulfill all his promises to us.

The *ultimate* instruction of the Torah for believers is to look for Jesus in its pages! Jesus said the Scriptures pointed to him (Luke 24:44). Reading the Torah is a continual adventure of seeking how the stories, laws, sacrifices, and poetry point to him!

A GUIDE TO READING, TEACHING, OR PREACHING THE TORAH

There are many ways to use the Torah as a discipleship manual. The Jewish rabbis[13] long ago developed a system for reading through the Torah aloud in a year in weekly synagogue meetings (there were 54 weeks in the ancient Jewish lunar calendar). I propose this as a helpful approach. Below is a table listing the weekly portions (*parashah/parsha*; plural *parashot*).

11. Leder, *Waiting*, 204. Leder cites Mauser, *Christ*, regarding the symbolism in Matthew 4 and Luke 4.

12. Wenham, *Pentateuch*, 155.

13. See https://en.wikipedia.org/wiki/Weekly_Torah_portion accessed January 27, 2020; adapted.

The table can be used for personal reading or for teaching or preaching the Torah. If one desires to read through the Torah in one year, simply divide each *parsha* portion into (say) five parts for a five-days-a-week Torah reading schedule. Since the *parsha* portions average two to six chapters a week, the readings are quite manageable when broken up over several days. Since there are 187 chapters in the Torah, the (say) 250 weekdays in a fifty-week year (you get two weeks of vacation!) means you can read the Torah in a year by reading less than one chapter a day! This makes it easy to read the Torah in a year. Or you can complete it more quickly.

Listening to the Torah on your phone is also an excellent way to cover the Torah! There are several advantages to this. One advantage is that *listening* is a change from our usual experience of reading the Bible and the experience is very different! Another is that it replicates what most believers until modern times experienced (since reading was not widespread): *hearing* Scripture. Importantly, since we often can listen when we drive, etc., listening often allows us to take in larger swaths of Scripture at a sitting. Covering larger portions at one time helps us to notice things we miss when we read small portions. A short road-trip might allow you to listen to an entire Torah book in one day! How the Apostle Paul would have loved that opportunity!

If one desires to go through the Torah in one year in a Sunday School class, or Bible study, or sermon series, the *parsha* portions will serve nicely (you must adjust for the Jewish 54-week calendar, perhaps by combining some smaller portions with others tangent to them). But if you wish to go at a slower pace, consider spending one year on a Torah book. Since there are ten to twelve *parsha* portions for each Torah book, it is not difficult to divide the book's *parsha* portions into about forty-eight or fifty smaller portions and cover a Torah book in a year. (Any commentary outline can help divide a book into appropriate units.)

The Bible's chapter divisions can also serve as the teaching/preaching units (though they are sometimes badly done: the creation story is Genesis 1:1—2:3!). Genesis's fifty chapters are better divided into sixty-eight teaching/preaching units,[14] but some combining of smaller passages can fit it into a year. You can also spend three months in a Torah book, take a break and come back, since the ear can only endure one type of biblical literature for a while.

14. I refer to Ross's divisions in *Creation and Blessing*.

Torah Book	Passage Number	*Parsha* Name	1-Year Reading/ Teaching/ Preaching *Parsha* portion
Genesis	1.	In the beginning	Gen 1:1—6:8
	2.	Noah (rest)	6:9—11:32
	3.	Go forth, yourself!	12:1—17:27
	4.	And he appeared	18:1—22:24
	5.	Life of Sarah	23:1—25:18
	6.	Generations	25:19—28:9
	7.	And he went out	28:10—32:3
	8.	And he sent	32:4—36:43
	9.	And he settled	37:1—40:23
	10.	At the end of	41:1—44:17
	11.	And he drew near	44:18—47:27
	12.	And he lived	47:28—50:26
Exodus	13.	Names	Exod 1:1—6:1
	14.	And I Appeared	6:2—9:35
	15.	Come!	10:1—13:16
	16.	When he sent out	13:17—17:16
	17.	Jethro	18:1—20:23
	18.	Laws	21:1—24:18
	19.	Offering	25:1—27:19
	20.	You shall command	27:20—30:10
	21.	When you elevate	30:11—34:35
	22.	And he assembled	35:1—38:20
	23.	Accountings	38:21—40:38
Leviticus	24.	And he called	Lev 1:1—5:26
	25.	Command!	6:1—8:36
	26.	Eighth	9:1—11:47
	27.	She bears seed	12:1—13:59
	28.	Infected one	14:1—15:33
	29.	After the death	16:1—18:30
	30.	Holy ones	19:1—20:27
	31.	Say gently	21:1—24:23
	32.	On the Mount	25:1—26:2
	33.	In My laws	26:3—27:34

Numbers	34.	In the wilderness	Num 1:1—4:20
	35.	Elevate!	4:21—7:89
	36.	In your uplifting	8:1—12:16
	37.	Send for yourself	13:1—15:41
	38.	Korach	16:1—18:32
	39.	Law	19:1—22:1
	40.	Balak	22:2—25:9
	41.	Phinehas	25:10—30:1
	42.	Tribes	30:2—32:42
	43.	Journeys of	33:1—36:13
Deuteronomy	44.	Words	Deut 1:1—3:22
	45.	Pleaded	3:23—7:11
	46.	As a result	7:12—11:25
	47.	See!	11:26—16:17
	48.	Judges	16:18—21:9
	49.	When you go out	21:10—25:19
	50.	When you enter in	26:1—29:8
	51.	Standing (Witnessing)	29:9—30:20
	52.	And he went	31:1—31:30
	53.	Listen!	32:1—32:52
	54.	And this is the blessing	33:1—34:12

HELPS FOR READING, TEACHING, AND PREACHING THE TORAH

Below are suggestions for books that will help you in reading the Torah, for teaching the Torah in a Sunday School class or a Bible study, or for preaching a sermon series though it. The books suggested are aimed at three things: (1) understanding the Torah, text by text; (2) seeing Jesus in the Torah; and (3) applying the Torah to the life of the believer. The books vary in which of these three they emphasize, and the list is annotated for maximum benefit. You need not agree with all the positions taken, but such views can make you think. The personal reading section below is the most basic. Here I assume no advanced knowledge of Scripture and no special training in biblical studies. The books I suggest should all be accessible to anyone. The teaching and preaching section goes deeper. Some books I have recommended for both. Some that are more detailed and technical I have suggested for preachers.

Helps for Personal Reading of the Torah

On the Whole Torah

Wenham, *Exploring . . . the Pentateuch.* This is a rich, section-by-section commentary on the Torah, besides an introductory chapter (very useful) and three ending chapters on scholarly Torah study (these will not interest most people.) The commentary occupies 125 pages. It is filled with perceptive observations, such as how the flood is a reversal of the creation account and how Noah is pictured as a second Adam. If you want to read the Torah in a year along with a brief book (less than a page a day!), this book will be immensely rewarding! Wenham would be a great book for your first trip through the Torah.

On the Torah Books

Wenham can give only a section-by-section overview. For a grasp of the message of each passage, application and seeing Jesus in the text, in a manageable, non-technical package, these are the most useful. I would recommend reading the commentary after reading, or with, the text.

Genesis: Kidner, *Genesis.* The book is 224 pages long. For Genesis I am suggesting two possibilities. Kidner is as excellent as he is brief. He explains the text with great insight, though not verse by verse. His comments take 180 pages, averaging three pages per chapter (the creation story is eleven pages). Kidner is always worth reading.

Ross, *Creation and Blessing,* is 750 pages, 600 of which is passage-by-passage exposition. Ross is a master of biblical narrative literature and is brilliant on Genesis! Each passage is outlined as he would teach/preach it and explains the details that are important for understanding the passage and its spiritual lesson, which is stated in one clear sentence at the end of each passage. Ross averages about nine pages per passage, *but* if you skip the (valuable) preparatory material and read only the "Development of the Exposition" section for each passage, you can cover each passage in three to seven pages. Ross is *the best* read on Genesis for reading, teaching or preaching the book. Sell all that you have and buy Ross!

Exodus: Alan Cole, *Exodus*, 239 pages. Like Kidner above, Cole is an excellent, brief commentary on Exodus. The Introduction is informative and stimulating. The comments on the text are first-rate! An outstanding companion to Exodus for your first time through the book.

Leviticus: Harrison, *Leviticus*, 252 pages. Again, two possibilities. Harrison explains the text well. He elucidates the structure, clarifies what is obscure, explains what we cannot be certain about, and points to Jesus in the text. He is quite detailed on ANE practices and their relation to the text and on medical issues (like "leprosy"). A fine guide to Leviticus.

Leviticus: Ross, *Holiness to the Lord*, 500 pages. Like Ross on Genesis; 400 pages of passage-by-passage exposition, averaging eight pages per passage. He states the spiritual lesson of the passage in one sentence at the end of each unit. Again, if you skip the (worthwhile) preparatory material and read only the "Development of the Exposition" and the "Concluding Observations" for each passage, you can cover each passage in, typically, five to six pages. Excellent!

Numbers: Wenham, *Numbers*, 240 pages. For Numbers, two possibilities. Wenham's brief commentary is outstanding! Meatier and less applicational than Duguid below (meaning is its focus), but a stellar guide to the meaning of Numbers and more compact than Duguid.

Duguid, *Numbers*, 400 pages. The 350 pages of passage-by-passage exposition average nine pages per passage. Engagingly written, Duguid's sermons are excellent on meaning, application, and seeing how the passages point to Jesus.

Deuteronomy: Thompson, *Deuteronomy*, 320 pages. After a thorough introduction, the commentary is 200 pages long. Thompson is especially strong on ANE backgrounds and he explains the text well.

Helps for Teaching and Preaching the Torah

On the Whole Torah

Sailhamer, *The Pentateuch as Narrative*, 522 pages. I would skip the Introduction; often fascinating, but hard to follow and often quite technical. The bulk of the book is a section-by-section commentary covering the Torah in detail. At 400 pages, it averages two pages per chapter of the Torah, but that varies widely. It is quite stimulating, explaining the meaning and often highlighting captivating literary features of the text, such as how "east" becomes symbolic of departure from God in Scripture, or pointing out foreshadowing.

Alexander, *From Paradise to Promised Land,* 360 pages. A fine treatment of the Torah, though not a commentary. The 200 pages covering Genesis through Deuteronomy (after a 100-page analysis of the Documentary hypothesis) devote chapters to seed, blessing, Passover, the tabernacle, sacrifice, etc., besides covering each book.

On the Torah Books

Genesis: Ross, *Creation and Blessing.* See the comments above under the "reading" section. Ross is *the best* single read on Genesis for reading, teaching, or preaching Genesis!

Waltke, Fredricks, *Genesis,* 600 pages. This commentary is rich in insight in only five to ten pages per chapter. Strong on structure, literary art, and theology.

Wenham, *Genesis 1–11* and *Genesis 12–50.* The volumes are 353 pages and 517 pages. This superb commentary is strong on detailed exegesis, exceptionally insightful, outstanding on literary artistry! Hebrew words are in Hebrew characters. For exegesis, not help in preaching.

Exodus: Enns, *Exodus,* 620 pages. The commentary on the text occupies 560 pages, averaging thirteen pages per chapter. Each section treats Original Meaning (detailed analysis), Bridging Contexts (interpreting the passage) and Contemporary Significance (application). For teaching you might skip the first section, cutting the pages in half to six or seven pages per section, but if you want details, turn to that section also. A very good commentary!

Stuart, *Exodus,* 827 pages. The actual commentary on the text is about 650 pages, or sixteen pages per chapter. It is expert, thorough, clear, and the discussions of Hebrew can generally be followed by anyone (Hebrew is transliterated, i.e., spelled in English letters). You will feel equipped to teach and answer questions when you have read Stuart.

Fretheim, *Exodus,* 321 pages. An excellent commentary for understanding and preaching the text, even though he argues throughout for God's changeability (the "Openness of God") and his endorsement of critical positions adds little to understanding or using the text.

Leviticus: Ross, *Holiness to the Lord,* 500 pages. Ross is *the best* single read on Leviticus for teaching and preaching the book, though he doesn't present as much technical information as Wenham or Hartley.

Wenham, *The Book of Leviticus,* 362 pages. Expert and relatively concise (eleven pages per chapter). Wenham is a master! Excellent!

Morales, *Theology of Leviticus*, 349 pages. Morales is not light reading but is a brilliant and engaging section-by-section analysis of the book. Excellent for exegesis, not preaching.

Hartley, *Leviticus*, 515 pages. Good detailed exegesis. Some moderate endorsements of documentary hypothesis positions.

Numbers: Wenham, *Numbers*, 240 pages. Excellent, just brief! A great help in understanding the book and preparing for teaching it.

Ashley, *Numbers*, 683 pages. Detailed exegesis, longer than Wenham and Cole.

Dennis Cole. *Numbers*, 352 pages. Detailed and useful.

Deuteronomy: Block, *Deuteronomy*, 880 pages. Try not to let the mammoth size scare you! The portion commenting on the text is 760 pages long, or an average of twenty-two pages per chapter. But since it is set up like Enns on Exodus (as all the NIVAC are), if you skip the Original Meaning section, you cut the pages to 40 percent of the total, meaning nine pages per chapter of Exodus. Unlike Merrill and Craigie below, Block deals with preaching the text.

Merrill, *Deuteronomy*, 477 pages. Excellent and organized around the suzerain-vassal structure. A bit more detailed than Craigie.

Craigie, *Deuteronomy*, 424 pages. Also excellent! Utilizes the suzerain-vassal structure.

Glossary

Aboth. A tractate in the Jewish Mishnah which means "[the sayings of the] Fathers."

ANE. Abbreviation for ancient Near East.

Apocrypha. Thirteen books or book portions included in the Catholic but not the Protestant OT.

Canon. The list of books included in a collection. For Jews and Christians, the list of books which constitute Scripture. The artillery gun which goes "boom" is a "cannon."

Cultus/cultic. Relating to the religious ceremonies of a group such as ancient Israel.

Documentary hypothesis. A theory developed in 1753 to explain oddities in the Torah text, such as late words (words not used in Moses' time), multiple ways of referring to God, and apparent repetitions. Theorizes there were four ancient sources called "J," "E," "D," and "P," believed to have been written over several centuries and eventually combined into the Torah.

External evidence. Information about something from a source outside of it, such as testimony from a witness about a book or event, e.g., the Jewish testimony that Moses wrote the Torah.

Former Prophets. The group of books in the Jewish arrangement of the Hebrew Bible which immediately follows the Torah. It includes Joshua, Judges, Samuel, and Kings.

Former Writings. A convenient way to refer to the first section of the "Writings" in the Jewish arrangement of the Hebrew Bible books, though not the common Jewish practice. It consists of Psalms, Job, Proverbs, Ruth, Song of Songs, Ecclesiastes, Lamentations, and Esther.

Hebrew Bible. The Bible of the Hebrews, that is, the Jewish Bible written in the Hebrew language, the literature Christians call "the Old Testament." Also, the Hebrew Bible in English.

Internal evidence. Information about something from the source itself. Regarding the Bible it includes what the Bible itself says, such as Isaiah saying it was written by Isaiah.

Kadesh-barnea. Place where Israel refused to enter Canaan due to fear (Numb 13–14).

Latter Prophets. The group of books in the Jewish arrangement of the Hebrew Bible which immediately follows the Former Prophets. It includes Isaiah, Jeremiah, Ezekiel and "the Twelve" (the Christian "Minor Prophets").

Latter Writings. A way to refer to the last section of the "Writings" in Hebrew Bible, though not the Jewish practice. It is composed of Daniel, Ezra-Nehemiah, and Chronicles.

Mishnah. Means two things. It refers primarily to the collection of the sayings of the Jewish rabbis from about 200 BC through AD 200, passed down orally from rabbi to pupil, then written down about AD 200. It is divided into six "Orders" such a Moed, and each Order has several tractates like *Aboth*. Each tractate is divided into chapters and each chapter into paragraphs. A paragraph is called a "Mishnah," the word's second meaning. The Jerusalem Talmud and Babylonian Talmud are much longer collections of rabbinic comments on the Mishnah, written about AD 350 and AD 500, respectively.

Pentateuch. A Christian name for the Torah, the five books traditionally attributed to Moses, Genesis, Exodus, Leviticus, Numbers, and Deuteronomy, from Greek, meaning "five scrolls."

Prophets. The group of books in the Jewish arrangement of the Hebrew Bible which immediately follows the Torah. It is composed of the "Former Prophets" and the "Latter Prophets." The arrangement dates to around 130 BC or before.

Propitiation. A NT term for the effect of Jesus' death (Romans 3:25) as satisfying God's wrath against sin and probably also the removing of our sins from us, both described in Lev 16.

Protoevangelium. A Latin word meaning "the first announcement of the gospel" (Genesis 3:15).

Septuagint. The translation of the Hebrew Bible into Greek in Alexandria, Egypt, beginning about 250 BC. Abbreviated "LXX." Because the NT authors wrote in Greek, they usually quoted the OT from the Septuagint rather than making their own translation from Hebrew.

Shema. A Hebrew imperative meaning "Hear!" and the first word in Deut 6:4, "Hear, O Israel, the Lord our God, the Lord is one." Because Jews see this as *the* foundational statement of monotheism ("one God"), Deut 6:4–5 was named "the *Shema*" for its first word, a common Jewish way of naming texts or documents. Observant Jews recite it every morning and evening.

Suzerain-vassal treaty. An ANE Hittite treaty form in which the conquering king (suzerain) stated the duties of the conquered people (vassal). The elements of Deuteronomy and their order match these treaties of 1400 BC and not later Assyrian ones, allowing Deuteronomy to be dated.

Tabernacle. The portable sacrifice and worship center where God's presence dwelt with Israel, built by Moses (Exod 25–40). It had an outer court, and inside a curtain, a holy place, and a holy of holies (Hebrew for "most holy place"). Eventually replaced by Solomon's temple.

Tanak. Jewish term for the Hebrew Bible, an acronym from the first letters of the Hebrew words for T*orah* (Law), N*ebi'im* (Prophets), and K*etubim* (Writings), with "a" added for pronunciation.

Temple. Solomon's permanent sacrifice and worship building which replaced the tabernacle.

Tent of Meeting. A name for the tabernacle emphasizing that it is where Israel met with God.

Theophany. An appearance of God in some visible form such as a cloud or a fire.

Torah. The Hebrew word meaning "instruction," sometimes "law," which became the name of the first section of the Hebrew Bible, Genesis, Exodus, Leviticus, Numbers, and Deuteronomy.

Tractate. A word derived from Latin meaning "treatise," "extended discussion," which came to be used for the sixty-three sections of the Jewish Mishnah, such as "*Aboth*."

Transjordan. The area occupied by Israel "across the Jordan" River from Canaan proper.

Writings. The books in the Jewish arrangement of the Hebrew Bible which immediately follow the Prophets, composed of what may be called the "Former Writings" and the "Latter Writings."

Bibliography

Aland, Kurt, et al., eds. *The Greek New Testament.* 3rd ed. New York: American Bible Society/United Bible Societies, 1983.

Aland, Kurt, et al., eds. *Novum Testamentum Graece/Nestle-Aland Greek Text.* 26th ed. Stuttgart: Deutsche Bibelgesellshaft, 1985.

Alden, Robert. "*Malachi.*" EBC. Edited by F. E. Gaebelein. Grand Rapids: Zondervan, 1976.

Alexander, T. D. "Authorship of the Pentateuch." In *DOTP* 61–72.

———. *From Paradise to Promised Land: An Introduction to the Pentateuch.* 3rd ed. Grand Rapids: Baker, 2012.

Alter, Robert. *The Art of Biblical Narrative.* Rev. ed. New York: Basic, 2011.

———. *The Five Books of Moses: A Translation with Commentary.* New York: Norton, 2004.

Ashley, Timothy R. *Numbers.* NICOT. Grand Rapids: Eerdmans, 1995.

Bar-Efrat, Shimon. *Narrative Art in the Bible.* Oxford: T & T Clark, 2004.

Beale. G. K. *Handbook on the New Testament Use of the Old Testament: Exegesis and Interpretation.* Grand Rapids: Baker, 2012.

———. *The Temple and the Church's Mission: A Biblical Theology of the Dwelling Place of God.* Downers Grove, IL: InterVarsity, 2004.

———. *A New Testament Theology: The Unfolding of the Old Testament in the New.* Grand Rapids, IL: Baker, 2011.

Beale. G. K., and Mitchell Kim. *God Dwells Among Us: Expanding Eden to the Ends of the Earth.* Downers Grove, IL: InterVarsity, 2014.

Beale. G. K., and Benjamin L. Gladd. *The Story Retold: A Biblical-Theological Introduction to the New Testament.* Downers Grove, IL: InterVarsity, 2020.

Beale. G. K., and D. A. Carson, eds. *Commentary on the New Testament Use of the Old Testament.* Grand Rapids: Baker, 2007.

Beckwith, Roger T. *The Old Testament Canon of the New Testament Church and its Background in Early Judaism.* Grand Rapids: Eerdmans, 1985.

Bird, Michael F. *Evangelical Theology: A Biblical and Systematic Introduction.* Grand Rapids: Zondervan, 2013.

Blackman, Philip, ed. *The Mishnah.* 7 vols. New York: Judaica, 1977.

Block, Daniel. *Deuteronomy.* NIVAC. Grand Rapids: Zondervan, 2012.

Bock, Darrell L. *Luke 9:51—24:53.* BECNT. Grand Rapids: Baker, 1996.

Bruce, F. F. *The Books and the Parchments.* Tappan, NJ: Revell, 1984.

———. *The Canon of Scripture*. Downers Grove, IL: InterVarsity, 1988.

———. *The Epistle to the Hebrews*. NICNT. Grand Rapids: Eerdmans, 1964.

Brueggemann, Walter. *Genesis*. IBC. Atlanta: John Knox, 1992.

Burgess, John. *After Baptism*. Louisville: Westminster John Knox, 2005.

Charry, Ellen T. *By the Renewing of Your Minds: The Pastoral Function of Christian Doctrine*. New York: Oxford University Press, 1997.

Childs, Brevard S. *Introduction to the Old Testament as Scripture*. Philadelphia: Fortress, 1979.

Clines, David J. A. *The Theme of the Pentateuch*. JSOTSup 10. Sheffield: JSOT, 1978.

Cole, Dennis. *Numbers*. NAC. Nashville, Broadman & Holman, 2000. Kindle.

Cole, R. Alan. *Exodus: An Introduction and Commentary*. TOTC. Downers Grove, IL: InterVarsity, 1973.

Coogan, Michael D., and Cynthia R. Chapman. *The Old Testament: A Historical and Literary Introduction to the Hebrew Scriptures*. 4th ed. New York: Oxford University Press, 2018.

Copan, Paul. *Is God a Moral Monster?* Grand Rapids: Baker, 2011.

Cowles, C. S., et al. *Show Them No Mercy: Four Views on God and Canaanite Genocide*. Grand Rapids: Zondervan, 2010.

Craigie, Peter C. *The Book of Deuteronomy*. NICOT. Grand Rapids: Eerdmans, 1976.

Daube, D. "Concessions to Sinfulness in Jewish Law." *Journal of Jewish Studies* 10 (1959) 1–13.

Dempster, Stephen G. *Dominion and Dynasty: A Theology of the Hebrew Bible*. Downers Grove, IL: InterVarsity, 2003.

———. "Torah, Torah, Torah: The Emergence of the Tripartite Canon." In *Exploring the Origins of the Bible: Canon Formation in Historical, Literary, and Theological Perspective*, edited by Craig A. Evans and Emanuel Tov, 87–127. Grand Rapids: Baker, 2008.

DeRouchie, Jason S. "The Blessing-Commission, the Promised Offspring, and the Toledot Structure of Genesis." *Journal of the Evangelical Theological Society* 56 (2013) 219–47.

———. *How to Understand and Apply the Old Testament: Twelve Steps from Exegesis to Theology*. Phillipsburg, NJ: P&R, 2017.

Dillard, Raymond B., and Tremper Longman III. *An Introduction to the Old Testament*. Grand Rapids: Zondervan, 1994.

Dodd, C. H. *According to the Scriptures: The Substructure of New Testament Theology*. London: Nisbet & Co., Ltd., 1952.

Dorsey, David A. *The Literary Structure of the Old Testament: A Commentary on Genesis to Malachi*. Grand Rapids: Baker, 1999.

Duguid, Ian M. *Numbers: God's Presence in the Wilderness*. Wheaton, IL: Crossway, 2006.

Duvall, J. Scott, and J. Daniel Hays. *God's Relational Presence: The Cohesive Center of Biblical Theology*. Grand Rapids: Baker, 2019.

Enns, Peter. *Exodus*. NIVAC. Grand Rapids: Zondervan, 2000.

Estelle, Bryan D. *Echoes of Exodus: Tracing a Biblical Motif*. Downers Grove, IL: InterVarsity, 2018.

Fee, Gordon D., and Douglas Stuart. *How to Read the Bible for All Its Worth*. 4th ed. Grand Rapids: Zondervan, 2014.

France, R. T. *The Gospel of Matthew*. NICNT. Grand Rapids: Eerdmans, 2007.

Fretheim, Terence E. *Exodus*. IBC. Louisville: John Knox, 1991.

———. "Exodus, Book of." In *DOTP* 248–58.

Gordon, T. David. *Promise, Law, Faith: Covenant-Historical Reasoning in Galatians*. Peabody, MA: Hendrickson, 2019.

Green, William Henry. *General Introduction to the Bible: The Canon*. Reprint, Grand Rapids: Baker, 1980.

Hamilton, Victor P. *The Book of Genesis, Chapters 1–17*. NICOT. Grand Rapids: Eerdmans, 2000.

Harrison, Roland Kenneth. *Introduction to the Old Testament*. Grand Rapids: Eerdmans, 1969.

———. *Leviticus: An Introduction and Commentary*. TOTC. Downers Grove, IL: InterVarsity, 1980.

Hart, Ian. "Genesis 1:1–2:3 as a Prologue to the Book of Genesis." *Tyndale Bulletin* 46 (1996) 315–36.

Hartley, John E. *Leviticus*. WBC. Dallas: Word, 1992. Kindle.

Harvey, John D. *Listening to the Text: Oral Patterning in Paul's Letters*. Grand Rapids: Baker, 1998.

Hopkins, Ezekiel. "Understanding the Ten Commandments." In *Classical Evangelical Essays in Old Testament Interpretation*, edited by Walter C. Kaiser Jr., 41–58. Grand Rapids: Baker, 1972.

Jobes, Karen H., and Moises Silva, ed. *Invitation to the Septuagint*. 2nd ed. Grand Rapids: Baker, 2015.

Kaiser, Walter C., Jr. *The Messiah in the Old Testament*. Grand Rapids: Zondervan, 1995.

———. *The Old Testament Documents: Are the Reliable and Relevant?* Downers Grove, IL: InterVarsity, 2001.

———. *The Promise—Plan of God: A Biblical Theology of the Old and New Testaments*. Grand Rapids: Zondervan, 2008.

———. *Toward an Exegetical Theology: Biblical Exegesis for Preaching and Teaching*. Grand Rapids: Baker, 1981.

———. *Toward an Old Testament Theology*. Grand Rapids: Zondervan, 1978.

———. *Toward Rediscovering the Old Testament*. Grand Rapids: Zondervan, 1978.

Kaiser, Walter C., Jr., ed. *Classical Evangelical Essays in Old Testament Interpretation*. Grand Rapids: Baker, 1972.

Kidner, Derek. *Genesis: An Introduction and Commentary*. TOTC. Downers Grove, IL: InterVarsity, 1967.

Kitchen, Kenneth A. *Ancient Orient and Old Testament*. Downers Grove, IL: InterVarsity, 1966.

———. *The Reliability of the Old Testament*. Grand Rapids: Eerdmans, 2003.

Lane, William. *The Gospel of Mark*. NICNT. Grand Rapids: Eerdmans, 1974.

———. *Hebrews 9–13*. WBC. Waco: Word, 1991. Kindle.

LaSor, William Sanford, et al. *Old Testament Survey: The Message, Form and Background of the Old Testament*. Grand Rapids: Eerdmans, 1982.

Leder, Arie C. *Waiting for the Land: The Story Line of the Pentateuch*. Phillipsburg, NJ: P&R, 2010.

Leithart, Peter J. *A House for My Name: A Survey of the Old Testament*. Moscow, ID: Canon, 2000.

Levinson, Bernard M. "Note on Deut 18:15." In *The Jewish Study Bible*, edited by Adele Berlin and Marc Zvi Brettler. Oxford: Oxford University Press, 2004.

Lewis, C. S. *The Last Battle*. Vol. 7 of *The Chronicles of Narnia*. New York: Macmillan, 1956.

———. *The Lion, the Witch and the Wardrobe*. Vol. 1 of *The Chronicles of Narnia*. New York: Macmillan, 1950.

———. *The Chronicles of Narnia*. 7 vols. New York: Macmillan, 1950–1956.

Lundbom, Jack. *Deuteronomy: A Commentary*. Grand Rapids: Eerdmans, 2013.

Mackie, Tim. *Read Scripture: Illustrated Summaries of Biblical Books*. Portland, OR: The Bible Project, 2017.

Margolis, Max. *The Hebrew Scriptures in the Making*. Philadelphia: Jewish Publication Society, 1922.

Mauser, Ulrich. *Christ in the Wilderness: The Wilderness Theme in the Second Gospel and its Basis in the Biblical Tradition*. Reprint, Eugene, OR: Wipf & Stock, 2009.

Mays, James Luther. *Psalms*. IBC. Louisville: John Knox, 1994.

McConville, Gordon J. "Covenant/*berit*." In *New International Dictionary of Old Testament Theology*, edited by Willem A. VanGemeren, 1:748. 5 vols. Grand Rapids: Zondervan, 1997.

McDonald, Lee Martin. *The Formation of the Christian Biblical Canon*. Nashville: Abingdon, 1988.

Merrill, Eugene H. *Deuteronomy*. NAC. Nashville, Broadman & Holman, 1994.

———. *Everlasting Dominion: A Theology of the Old Testament*. Nashville: Broadman & Holman, 2006.

———. "A Theology of the Pentateuch." In *A Biblical Theology of the Old Testament*, edited by Roy B. Zuck, consulting editors Eugene H. Merrill and Darrell L. Bock, 7–87. Chicago: Moody, 1991.

Merrill, Eugene H., et al. *The Word and the World: An Introduction to the Old Testament*. Nashville: Broadman & Holman, 2011.

Milgrom, Jacob, *Leviticus: A Continental Commentary*. Minneapolis: Fortress, 2004.

———. *Leviticus 1–16: A New Translation with Introduction and Commentary*. AB. New York: Doubleday, 1991.

———. *Numbers*. JPSTC. Philadelphia, Pennsylvania: Jewish Publication Society, 1989.

Morales, L. Michael. *Who Shall Ascend the Mountain of the Lord? A Biblical Theology of the Book of Leviticus*. Downers Grove, IL: InterVarsity, 2015.

Neusner, Jacob. "Torah." In *Dictionary of Judaism in the Biblical Period: 450 B.C.E. to 600 C.E.*, edited by Jaacob Neusner and William Scott Green, 637. Reprint, Peabody, MA: Hendrickson, 1999.

New American Bible Revised ed. Nashville: Catholic Bible Press, 1987.

Olson, Dennis T. *The Death of the Old and the Birth of the New: The Framework of the Book of Numbers and the Pentateuch*. Brown Judaic Studies 71. Chico, California: Scholars, 1985.

———. *Numbers*. IBC. Louisville: Westminster John Knox, 1996.

Packer, J. I. *Lord, I Want to be a Christian*. London: Kingsway, 1977.

Poythress, Vern. *The Shadow of Christ in the Law of Moses*. Phillipsburg, NJ: P&R, 1991.

Rad, Gerhard von. *Genesis: A Commentary*. Rev. ed. Philadelphia: Westminster, 1972.

Ross, Allen P. *A Commentary on the Psalms*. 3 vols. Grand Rapids: Kregel, 2011–2016.

———. *Creation and Blessing: A Guide to the Study and Exposition of Genesis*. Grand Rapids: Baker, 1998.

———. *Holiness to the Lord: A Guide to the Exposition of the Book of Leviticus*. Grand Rapids: Baker, 2006.

Sailhamer, John H. *Introduction to Old Testament Theology: A Canonical Approach.* Grand Rapids: Zondervan, 1995.

———. *The Meaning of the Pentateuch: Revelation, Composition and Interpretation.* Downers Grove: InterVarsity, 2009.

———. *The Pentateuch as Narrative: A Biblical-Theological Commentary.* Grand Rapids: Zondervan, 1992.

Stark, Rodney. *America's Blessings: How Religion Benefits Everyone, including Atheists.* West Conshohocken, PA: Templeton, 2012.

Stuart, Douglas K. *Exodus.* NAC Nashville: Broadman & Holman, 2006.

———. *Hosea-Jonah.* WBC. Grand Rapids: Zondervan, 1988. Kindle.

Thompson, J. A. *1 and 2 Chronicles.* NAC. Nashville: Broadman & Holman, 1994. Kindle.

———. *Deuteronomy: An Introduction and Commentary.* TOTC. Downers Grove, IL: InterVarsity, 1974.

Tierney, John, and Roy F. Baumeister. "For the New Year, Say No to Negativity." *Wall Street Journal*, December 27, 2019.

Waite, Linda J., and Maggie Gallagher. *The Case for Marriage: Why Married People are Happier, Healthier, and Better off Financially.* New York: Doubleday, 2000.

Waltke, Bruce K., with Cathi J. Fredricks. *Genesis: A Commentary.* Grand Rapids: Zondervan, 2001.

Waltke, Bruce K., with Charles Yu. *An Old Testament Theology: An Exegetical, Canonical, and Thematic Approach.* Grand Rapids: Zondervan, 2007.

Wenham, G. J. *The Book of Leviticus.* NICOT. Grand Rapids: Eerdmans, 1979.

———. "The Deuteronomic Theology of the Book of Joshua." *Journal of Biblical Literature* 90 (1971) 140–48.

———. *Exploring the Old Testament: Volume 1: A Guide to the Pentateuch.* Downers Grove, IL: InterVarsity: 2003.

———. *Genesis 1–15.* WBC. Dallas: Word, 1987.

———. *Genesis 16–50.* WBC. Dallas: Word, 1994.

———. *Numbers: An Introduction and Commentary.* TOTC. Downers Grove, IL: InterVarsity, 1981.

Wenham, John. *Christ and the Bible.* Grand Rapids: Baker, 1994.

Westermann, Claus. *Genesis 12–36.* A Continental Commentary. Translated by John J. Scullion. Minneapolis: Fortress, 1995.

Whybray, R. N. *The Making of the Pentateuch: A Methodological Study.* Sheffield: JSOT, 1987.

Wiseman, P. J. *Ancient Records and the Structure of Genesis: A Case for Literary Unity.* Nashville: Nelson, 1985.

CPSIA information can be obtained
at www.ICGtesting.com
Printed in the USA
BVHW071408080820
585889BV00004B/15